MACBETH

MACBETH

William Shakespeare

WORDSWORTH CLASSICS

This edition published 1992
by Wordsworth Editions Limited
Cumberland House, Crib Street, Ware,
Hertfordshire SG12 9ET

ISBN 1-57335-378-7

*Printed and bound in Great Britain
by Mackays of Chatham plc, Chatham, Kent*

Introduction

MACBETH (1605-6) was written by Shakespeare when he was at the height of his powers; *Hamlet*, *King Lear* and *Othello* were written in the years immediately preceding it, and these four plays are counted as the greatest of the Shakespearean tragedies.

The story was freely adapted from Holinshed's *Chronicles*, and the subject was chosen as a compliment to the new King James I (of England) and VI (of Scotland). As well as its Scottish setting, it incorporates the tradition that James was descended from Banquo, and also aspects of the supernatural, in which James took so great an interest. Although the play was 'politically correct' for its time, Shakespeare uses these elements to enhance his imaginative attention, and the play exemplifies one of the beliefs of Shakespeare's time that where evil breaks into the soul of a king, evil will extend over the state ruled by that king.

In contrast to Hamlet, a man of ideas and inaction, Macbeth is a man of ambition and vigorous action. As the play opens, Macbeth is seen as the defender of Scotland against the triple alliance of the King of Norway, the rebel Macdonwald and the secret rebel, the Thane of Cawdor. Returning from his victory over this alliance, Macbeth meets three witches who foretell a great future for the general – that he will be Thane of Cawdor, and King hereafter. Of Macbeth's colleague, Banquo, the witches prophesy that he will be the ancestor of all kings. When reunited with his wife, Macbeth is overwhelmed by another triple alliance, that of the witches' prophesies, his own ambitions and those of Lady Macbeth.

Macbeth's ambition is sparked into flame when King Duncan grants Macbeth the disgraced Cawdor's lands and title, and he sees the beginning of the fulfillment of the witches' prophesies. Lady Macbeth, too, sees the pattern emerging, and persuades her husband that the only way forward is to murder Duncan as he sleeps. Hesitantly and rather reluctantly Macbeth complies with his wife's urgings, stabbing the King in his bedchamber. In the chaotic aftermath of the murder's discovery, Duncan's two sons escape, and in due course Macbeth is hailed as King. However, Macbeth discovers that he is now sucked into a vortex of violence from which there is no escape. To ensure Banquo's descendants do not succeed to the throne, Macbeth arranges for Banquo's murder – but his son escapes the incompetant ambush. Haunted by Banquo's ghost and compelled to continue in his cruel tyranny 'I am in blood stepped in so far, that should I wade no more, returning were as tedious as go o'er', Macbeth's rule and Lady Macbeth's tormented soul crack under the strain. As an English army with Duncan's sons in attendance approach Macbeth's castle, Lady Macbeth commits suicide, and in the subsequent battle, Macbeth is killed.

Details of Shakespeare's early life are scanty. He was born the son of a prosperous merchant of Stratford-upon-Avon, and tradition has it that he was born on 23rd April 1564; records show that he was baptized three days later. It is likely that he attended the local grammar school, but he had no university education. Of his early career there is no record, though John Aubrey states that he was, for a time, a country schoolmaster. How he became involved with the stage is equally uncertain, but he was sufficiently established as a playwright by 1592 to be criticised in print. He was a leading member of the Lord Chamberlain's company, which became the King's Men on the accession of James I in 1603. Shakespeare married Anne Hathaway in 1582, by whom he had two daughters and a son, Hamnet, who died in childhood. Towards the end of his life he loosened his ties with London, and retired to New Place, his substantial property in Stratford that he had bought in 1597. He died on 23rd April 1616 aged 52, and is buried in Holy Trinity Church, Stratford.

Further reading:
A.C. Bradley: *Shakespearean Tragedy* 1904
M. McElroy: *Shakespeare's Mature Tragedies* 1973
M. Mack: *Killing the King: Three
    Studies in Shakespeare's Tragic Structure* 1973
M.N. Proser: *The Heroic Image in Five Shakespearean Tragedies* 1965
J. Thurber: *My World and Welcome to It: The Macbeth
    Murder Mystery* 1945

MACBETH

MACBETH

MACBETH

[1. 1.] *'Thunder and lightning. Enter three Witches'*

1 *Witch*. When shall we three meet again
In thunder, lightning, or in rain?
2 *Witch*. When the hurlyburly's done,
When the battle's lost and won.
3 *Witch*. That will be ere the set of sun.
1 *Witch*. Where the place?
2 *Witch*.   Upon the heath.
3 *Witch*. There to meet with Macbeth.
1 *Witch*. I come, Graymalkin!
2 *Witch*. Paddock calls.
3 *Witch*. Anon!   10
All. Fair is foul, and foul is fair:
Hover through the fog and filthy air.

[*they vanish in mist*

[1. 2.]   *A camp*

'Alarum.' 'Enter King' DUNCAN, *'*MALCOLM, DONAL-
BAIN, LENNOX, *with attendants, meeting a bleeding
Captain'*

Duncan. What bloody man is that? He can report,
As seemeth by his plight, of the revolt
The newest state.
Malcolm.   This is the sergeant,
Who like a good and hardy soldier fought
'Gainst my captivity...Hail, brave friend!
Say to the king the knowledge of the broil
As thou didst leave it.

   Captain.   Doubtful it stood,
As two spent swimmers that do cling together
And choke their art. . . The merciless Macdonwald
10 (Worthy to be a rebel, for to that
The multiplying villainies of nature
Do swarm upon him) from the Western Isles
Of kerns and gallowglasses is supplied,
And Fortune, on his damnéd quarrel smiling,
Showed like a rebel's whore: but all's too weak:
For brave Macbeth (well he deserves that name)
Disdaining fortune, with his brandished steel,
Which smoked with bloody execution,
Like Valour's minion carvéd out his passage,
20 Till he faced the slave;
Which ne'er shook hands, nor bade farewell
      to him,
Till he unseamed him from the nave to th' chops,
And fixed his head upon our battlements.
   Duncan. O, valiant cousin! worthy gentleman!
   Captain. As whence the sun 'gins his reflection
Shipwracking storms and direful thunders break;
So from that spring whence comfort seemed to come
Discomfort swells: mark, king of Scotland, mark!
No sooner justice had, with valour armed,
30 Compelled these skipping kerns to trust their heels,
But the Norweyan lord, surveying vantage,
With furbished arms and new supplies of men,
Began a fresh assault.
   Duncan.   Dismayed not this
Our captains, Macbeth and Banquo?
   Captain.   Yes;
As sparrows, eagles; or the hare, the lion.
If I say sooth, I must report they were
As cannons overcharged with double cracks;

So they
Doubly redoubled strokes upon the foe:
Except they meant to bathe in reeking wounds,   40
Or memorize another Golgotha,
I cannot tell:
But I am faint, my gashes cry for help.
  Duncan. So well thy words become thee as thy
    wounds,
They smack of honour both: Go get him surgeons.
                          [*attendants help him thence*
Who comes here?

'*Enter* Ross *and* Angus'

  Malcolm.   The worthy thane of Ross.
  Lennox. What a haste looks through his eyes! So
    should he look
That seems to speak things strange.
  Ross.   God save the king!
  Duncan. Whence cam'st thou, worthy thane?
  Ross.   From Fife, great king,
Where the Norweyan banners flout the sky,   50
And fan our people cold.
Norway himself, with terrible numbers,
Assisted by that most disloyal traitor
The thane of Cawdor, began a dismal conflict,
Till that Bellona's bridegroom, lapped in proof,
Confronted him with self-comparisons,
Point against point, rebellious arm 'gainst arm,
Curbing his lavish spirit: and, to conclude,
The victory fell on us.
  Duncan.   Great happiness!
  Ross. That now   60
Sweno, the Norways' king, craves composition;
Nor would we deign him burial of his men

Till he disbursèd, at Saint Colme's Inch,
Ten thousand dollars to our general use.

Duncan. No more that thane of Cawdor shall deceive
Our bosom interest: go pronounce his present death,
And with his former title greet Macbeth.

Ross. I'll see it done.

Duncan. What he hath lost, noble Macbeth hath won.

[they go

[**I. 3.**]　　　　　　　*A barren heath*

'*Thunder. Enter the three Witches*'

1 *Witch.* Where hast thou been, sister?

2 *Witch.* Killing swine.

3 *Witch.* Sister, where thou?

1 *Witch.* A sailor's wife had chestnuts in her lap,
And munched, and munched, and munched: 'Give
　　me', quoth I.
'Aroint thee, witch!' the rump-fed ronyon cries.
Her husband's to Aleppo gone, master o'th' Tiger:
But in a sieve I'll thither sail,
And, like a rat without a tail,
10 I'll do, I'll do, and I'll do.

2 *Witch.* I'll give thee a wind.

1 *Witch.* Th'art kind.

3 *Witch.* And I another.

1 *Witch.* I myself have all the other,
And the very ports they blow,
All the quarters that they know
I'th' shipman's card.
I will drain him dry as hay:
Sleep shall, neither night nor day
20 Hang upon his pent-house lid;
He shall live a man forbid:

Weary sev'nights nine times nine
Shall he dwindle, peak, and pine:
Though his bark cannot be lost,
Yet it shall be tempest-tost.
Look what I have.
    2 *Witch.* Show me, show me.
    1 *Witch.* Here I have a pilot's thumb,
Wrecked as homeward he did come.   ['*drum within*'
    3 *Witch.* A drum, a drum!   30
Macbeth doth come.

They dance in a ring, whirling faster and faster

    All. The Weïrd Sisters, hand in hand,
Posters of the sea and land,
Thus do go, about, about,
Thrice to thine, and thrice to mine,
And thrice again, to make up nine.
Peace! the charm's wound up.
                [*they stop suddenly, and a mist hides them*

'*Enter MACBETH and BANQUO*'

    Macbeth. So foul and fair a day I have not seen.
    Banquo. How far is't called to Forres?   [*the mist
        thins*] What are these,
So withered, and so wild in their attire,   40
That look not like th'inhabitants o'th'earth,
And yet are on't? Live you? or are you aught
That man may question? You seem to understand me,
By each at once her choppy finger laying
Upon her skinny lips: you should be women,
And yet your beards forbid me to interpret
That you are so.
    Macbeth.   Speak, if you can: what are you?

1 *Witch*. All hail, Macbeth! hail to thee, thane of
    Glamis!

2 *Witch*. All hail, Macbeth! hail to thee, thane of
    Cawdor!

50 3 *Witch*. All hail, Macbeth! that shalt be king
    hereafter.

Banquo. Good sir, why do you start, and seem to
    fear

Things that do sound so fair? I'th' name of truth,

Are ye fantastical, or that indeed

Which outwardly ye show? My noble partner

You greet with present grace and great prediction

Of noble having and of royal hope,

That he seems rapt withal: to me you speak not.

If you can look into the seeds of time,

And say which grain will grow and which will not,

60 Speak then to me, who neither beg nor fear

Your favours nor your hate.

1 *Witch*. Hail!

2 *Witch*. Hail!

3 *Witch*. Hail!

1 *Witch*. Lesser than Macbeth, and greater.

2 *Witch*. Not so happy, yet much happier.

3 *Witch*. Thou shalt get kings, though thou be
    none:

So all hail, Macbeth and Banquo!

1 *Witch*. Banquo and Macbeth, all hail!

                               [the mist thickens

70 *Macbeth*. Stay, you imperfect speakers, tell me more:

By Sinel's death I know I am thane of Glamis,

But how of Cawdor? the thane of Cawdor lives

A prosperous gentleman; and to be king

Stands not within the prospect of belief,

No more than to be Cawdor. Say from whence

You owe this strange intelligence, or why
Upon this blasted heath you stop our way
With such prophetic greeting. Speak, I charge you.

                                    [*they disappear*

  Banquo. The earth hath bubbles, as the water has,
And these are of them: whither are they vanished?   80
  Macbeth. Into the air; and what seemed corporal,
          melted,
As breath into the wind. Would they had stayed!
  Banquo. Were such things here as we do speak about?
Or have we eaten on the insane root
That takes the reason prisoner?
  Macbeth. Your children shall be kings.
  Banquo.   You shall be king.
  Macbeth. And thane of Cawdor too: went it not so?
  Banquo. To th' selfsame tune and words. Who's here?

'*Enter Ross and Angus*'

  Ross. The king hath happily received, Macbeth,
The news of thy success: and when he reads   90
Thy personal venture in the rebels' fight,
His wonders and his praises do contend
Which should be thine or his: silenced with that,
In viewing o'er the rest o'th' self-same day,
He finds thee in the stout Norweyan ranks,
Nothing afeard of what thyself didst make
Strange images of death. As thick as hail
Came post with post, and every one did bear
Thy praises in his kingdom's great defence,
And poured them down before him.
  Angus.   . We are sent   100
To give thee from our royal master thanks,
Only to herald thee into his sight,
Not pay thee.

Ross. And for an earnest of a greater honour,
He bade me, from him, call thee thane of Cawdor:
In which addition, hail, most worthy thane,
For it is thine.

Banquo.   What, can the devil speak true?

Macbeth. The thane of Cawdor lives: why do you
    dress me
In borrowed robes?

Angus.   Who was the thane lives yet,
110 But under heavy judgment bears that life
Which he deserves to lose. Whether he was combined
With those of Norway, or did line the rebel
With hidden help and vantage, or that with both
He laboured in his country's wreck, I know not;
But treasons capital, confessed, and proved,
Have overthrown him.

  (*Macbeth.*   Glamis, and thane of Cawdor:
The greatest is behind.—[*aloud*] Thanks for your
    pains—
[*aside to Banquo*] Do you not hope your children shall
    be kings,
When those that gave the thane of Cawdor to me
120 Promised no less to them?

Banquo.   That, trusted home,
Might yet enkindle you unto the crown,
Besides the thane of Cawdor. But 'tis strange:
And oftentimes, to win us to our harm,
The instruments of darkness tell us truths,
Win us with honest trifles, to betray's
In deepest consequence.
Cousins, a word, I pray you.

                [*to Ross and Angus, who move towards him*
  (*Macbeth.*   Two truths are told,
As happy prologues to the swelling act

Of the imperial theme. [*aloud*] I thank you, gentle-
          men.
[*aside*] This supernatural soliciting   130
Cannot be ill; cannot be good. If ill,
Why hath it given me earnest of success,
Commencing in a truth? I am thane of Cawdor.
If good, why do I yield to that suggestion
Whose horrid image doth unfix my hair,
And make my seated heart knock at my ribs,
Against the use of nature? Present fears
Are less than horrible imaginings:
My thought, whose murder yet is but fantastical,
Shakes so my single state of man that function   140
Is smothered in surmise, and nothing is
But what is not.
     Banquo.   Look how our partner's rapt.
     (*Macbeth*. If chance will have me king, why, chance
          may crown me,
Without my stir.
     Banquo.   New honours come upon him,
Like our strange garments, cleave not to their mould
But with the aid of use.
     (*Macbeth*.   Come what come may,
Time and the hour runs through the roughest day.
     Banquo. Worthy Macbeth, we stay upon your leisure.
     Macbeth. Give me your favour: my dull brain was
          wrought
With things forgotten. Kind gentlemen, your pains   150
Are registered where every day I turn
The leaf to read them....Let us toward the king.
                         [*aside to Banquo*
Think upon what hath chanced; and at more time,
The interim having weighed it, let us speak
Our free hearts each to other.

Banquo.   Very gladly.
Macbeth. Till then, enough.... Come, friends.
                              [they go forward

[1. 4.]   *Forres. A Room in the Palace*

    '*Flourish. Enter King*' DUNCAN, '*MALCOLM,
       DONALBAIN, LENNOX, and Attendants*'

Duncan. Is execution done on Cawdor? Are not
Those in commission yet returned?
   Malcolm.   My liege,
They are not yet come back. But I have spoke
With one that saw him die: who did report
That very frankly he confessed his treasons,
Implored your highness' pardon, and set forth
A deep repentance: nothing in his life
Became him like the leaving it; he died
As one that had been studied in his death,
10 To throw away the dearest thing he owed
As 'twere a careless trifle.
   Duncan.   There's no art
To find the mind's construction in the face:
He was a gentleman on whom I built
An absolute trust.

   '*Enter MACBETH, BANQUO, ROSS, and ANGUS*'

                O worthiest cousin!
The sin of my ingratitude even now
Was heavy on me. Thou art so far before,
That swiftest wing of recompense is slow
To overtake thee. Would thou hadst less deserved,
That the proportion both of thanks and payment
20 Might have been mine! only I have left to say,
More is thy due than more than all can pay.

Macbeth. The service and the loyalty I owe,
In doing it, pays itself. Your highness' part
Is to receive our duties: and our duties
Are to your throne and state children and servants;
Which do but what they should, by doing every thing
Safe toward your love and honour.
  Duncan.   Welcome hither:
I have begun to plant thee, and will labour
To make thee full of growing. Noble Banquo,
That hast no less deserved, nor must be known   30
No less to have done so: let me infold thee,
And hold thee to my heart.
  Banquo.   There if I grow,
The harvest is your own.
  Duncan.   My plenteous joys,
Wanton in fulness, seek to hide themselves
In drops of sorrow....Sons, kinsmen, thanes,
And you whose places are the nearest, know,
We will establish our estate upon
Our eldest, Malcolm, whom we name hereafter
The Prince of Cumberland: which honour must
Not unaccompanied invest him only,   40
But signs of nobleness, like stars, shall shine
On all deservers....From hence to Inverness,
And bind us further to you.
  Macbeth. The rest is labour, which is not used for
    you:
I'll be myself the harbinger, and make joyful
The hearing of my wife with your approach;
So humbly take my leave.
  Duncan.   My worthy Cawdor!
  (*Macbeth.* The Prince of Cumberland! that is a step
On which I must fall down, or else o'er-leap,
For in my way it lies. Stars, hide your fires!   50

Let not light see my black and deep desires:
The eye wink at the hand; yet let that be
Which the eye fears, when it is done, to see.   [*he goes*
 Duncan. True, worthy Banquo; he is full so valiant,
And in his commendations I am fed;
It is a banquet to me. Let's after him,
Whose care is gone before to bid us welcome:
It is a peerless kinsman.   ['*Flourish.*' *They go*

[1. 5.]   *Inverness. Before Macbeth's castle*

'*Enter MACBETH's wife alone, with a letter*'

Lady M. [*reads*] 'They met me in the day of success;
and I have learned by the perfect'st report, they have
more in them than mortal knowledge. When I burned
in desire to question them further, they made themselves
air, into which they vanished. Whiles I stood rapt in
the wonder of it, came missives from the king, who all-
hailed me, 'Thane of Cawdor', by which title, before,
these Weïrd Sisters saluted me, and referred me to the
coming on of time, with 'Hail, king that shalt be!' This
10 have I thought good to deliver thee (my dearest partner
of greatness) that thou mightst not lose the dues of
rejoicing, by being ignorant of what greatness is
promised thee. Lay it to thy heart, and farewell.'
Glamis thou art, and Cawdor, and shalt be
What thou art promised: yet do I fear thy nature,
It is too full o'th' milk of human kindness
To catch the nearest way: thou wouldst be great,
Art not without ambition, but without
The illness should attend it: what thou wouldst highly,
20 That wouldst thou holily; wouldst not play false,

And yet wouldst wrongly win: thou'ldst have, great
　　Glamis,
That which cries 'Thus thou must do', if thou have it,
And that which rather thou dost fear to do
Than wishest should be undone. Hie thee hither,
That I may pour my spirits in thine ear,
And chastise with the valour of my tongue
All that impedes thee from the golden round,
Which fate and metaphysical aid doth seem
To have thee crowned withal.

An attendant enters

　　　　　　　　　What is your tidings?
Attendant. The king comes here to-night.
Lady M. 　　　　　　　Thou'rt mad to say it! 30
Is not thy master with him? who, were't so,
Would have informed for preparation.
Attendant. So please you, it is true: our thane is
　　coming:
One of my fellows had the speed of him;
Who, almost dead for breath, had scarcely more
Than would make up his message.
Lady M. 　　　　　　　Give him tending,
He brings great news. [*attendant goes*] The raven
　　himself is hoarse
That croaks the fatal entrance of Duncan
Under my battlements....Come, you spirits
That tend on mortal thoughts, unsex me here, 　　　40
And fill me, from the crown to the toe, top-full
Of direst cruelty! make thick my blood,
Stop up th'access and passage to remorse,
That no compunctious visitings of nature
Shake my fell purpose, nor keep peace between
Th'effect and it! Come to my woman's breasts,

And take my milk for gall, you murd'ring ministers,
Wherever in your sightless substances
You wait on nature's mischief! Come, thick night,
50 And pall thee in the dunnest smoke of hell,
That my keen knife see not the wound it makes,
Nor heaven peep through the blanket of the dark,
To cry 'Hold, hold!'

'Enter MACBETH'

Great Glamis! worthy Cawdor!
Greater than both, by the all-hail hereafter!
Thy letters have transported me beyond
This ignorant present, and I feel now
The future in the instant.
   Macbeth.   My dearest love,
Duncan comes here to-night.
   Lady M.   And when goes hence?
   Macbeth. To-morrow, as he purposes.
   Lady M.   O, never
60 Shall sun that morrow see!
Your face, my thane, is as a book, where men
May read strange matters. To beguile the time,
Look like the time, bear welcome in your eye,
Your hand, your tongue: look like th'innocent flower,
But be the serpent under't. He that's coming
Must be provided for: and you shall put
This night's great business into my dispatch,
Which shall to all our nights and days to come
Give solely sovereign sway and masterdom.
70 *Macbeth*. We will speak further.
   Lady M.   Only look up clear:
To alter favour ever is to fear:
Leave all the rest to me.   *[they go within*

[1. 6.] *'Hautboys.' 'Enter King' DUNCAN, 'MALCOLM,
DONALBAIN, BANQUO, LENNOX, MACDUFF, ROSS,
ANGUS, and attendants'*

  Duncan. This castle hath a pleasant seat; the air
Nimbly and sweetly recommends itself
Unto our gentle senses.

  Banquo.   This guest of summer,
The temple-haunting martlet, does approve,
By his loved mansionry, that the heaven's breath
Smells wooingly here: no jutty, frieze,
Buttress, nor coign of vantage, but this bird
Hath made his pendent bed and procreant cradle:
Where they most breed and haunt, I have observed
The air is delicate.

         'Enter LADY' MACBETH

  Duncan.   See, see! our honoured hostess!   10
The love that follows us sometime is our trouble,
Which still we thank as love. Herein I teach you
How you shall bid God 'ield us for your pains,
And thank us for your trouble.

  Lady M.   All our service
In every point twice done, and then done double,
Were poor and single business to contend
Against those honours deep and broad, wherewith
Your majesty loads our house: for those of old,
And the late dignities heaped up to them,
We rest your hermits.

  Duncan.   Where's the thane of Cawdor? 20
We coursed him at the heels, and had a purpose
To be his purveyor: but he rides well,
And his great love (sharp as his spur) hath holp him
To his home before us. Fair and noble hostess,
We are your guest to-night.

Lady M.   Your servants ever
Have theirs, themselves, and what is theirs, in compt,
To make their audit at your highness' pleasure,
Still to return your own.
    Duncan.   Give me your hand:
Conduct me to mine host; we love him highly,
30 And shall continue our graces towards him.
By your leave, hostess.   [*he conducts her into the castle*

[1. 7.] *A court in Macbeth's castle, open to the sky, with
doors to the rear, one on the left the main gate or south
entry, one on the right leading to rooms within, and between
them a covered recess running back, beneath a gallery, to a
third door, through the which when ajar may be seen a flight
of stairs to an upper chamber. A bench with a table before
it against a side wall.*

   '*Hautboys. Torches. Enter a sewer*' *directing* '*divers
servants*' *who pass* '*with dishes and service*' *across the
court. As they come through the door on the right a sound
of feasting is heard within.* '*Then enter* MACBETH' *from
the same door*

   Macbeth. If it were done, when 'tis done, then 'twere
      well
It were done quickly: if th'assassination
Could trammel up the consequence, and catch,
With his surcease, success; that but this blow
Might be the be-all and the end-all....here,
But here, upon this bank and shoal of time,
We'ld jump the life to come. But in these cases
We still have judgement here—that we but teach
Bloody instructions, which being taught return
10 To plague th'inventor: this even-handed justice
Commends th'ingredience of our poisoned chalice

To our own lips. He's here in double trust:
First, as I am his kinsman and his subject,
Strong both against the deed; then, as his host,
Who should against his murderer shut the door,
Not bear the knife myself. Besides, this Duncan
Hath borne his faculties so meek, hath been
So clear in his great office, that his virtues
Will plead like angels, trumpet-tongued, against
The deep damnation of his taking-off: 20
And pity, like a naked new-born babe,
Striding the blast, or Heaven's cherubin, horsed
Upon the sightless couriers of the air,
Shall blow the horrid deed in every eye,
That tears shall drown the wind. I have no spur
To prick the sides of my intent, but only
Vaulting ambition, which o'erleaps itself,
And falls on th'other—

'*Enter LADY*' MACBETH

                              How now, what news?
Lady M. He has almost supped: why have you left
      the chamber?
Macbeth. Hath he asked for me?
Lady M.   Know you not he has? 30
Macbeth. We will proceed no further in this business:
He hath honoured me of late, and I have bought
Golden opinions from all sorts of people,
Which would be worn now in their newest gloss,
Not cast aside so soon.
Lady M.   Was the hope drunk
Wherein you dressed yourself? hath it slept since?
And wakes it now, to look so green and pale
At what it did so freely? From this time
Such I account thy love. Art thou afeard

40   To be the same in thine own act and valour
As thou art in desire? Wouldst thou have that
Which thou esteem'st the ornament of life,
And live a coward in thine own esteem,
Letting 'I dare not' wait upon 'I would',
Like the poor cat i'th'adage?

    Macbeth.   Prithee, peace:
I dare do all that may become a man;
Who dares do more, is none.

    Lady M.   What beast was't then
That made you break this enterprise to me?
When you durst do it, then you were a man;
50   And, to be more than what you were, you would
Be so much more the man. Nor time nor place
Did then adhere, and yet you would make both:
They have made themselves, and that their fitness
      now
Does unmake you. I have given suck, and know
How tender 'tis to love the babe that milks me—
I would, while it was smiling in my face,
Have plucked my nipple from his boneless gums,
And dashed the brains out, had I so sworn as you
Have done to this.

    Macbeth.   If we should fail?
    Lady M.   We fail?
60   But screw your courage to the sticking place,
And we'll not fail. When Duncan is asleep
(Whereto the rather shall his day's hard journey
Soundly invite him) his two chamberlains
Will I with wine and wassail so convince,
That memory, the warder of the brain,
Shall be a fume, and the receipt of reason
A limbec only: when in swinish sleep
Their drenchéd natures lie as in a death,

What cannot you and I perform upon
Th'unguarded Duncan? what not put upon   70
His spongy officers, who shall bear the guilt
Of our great quell?

Macbeth.   Bring forth men-children only!
For thy undaunted mettle should compose
Nothing but males. Will it not be received,
When we have marked with blood those sleepy two
Of his own chamber, and used their very daggers,
That they have done't?

Lady M.   Who dares receive it other,
As we shall make our griefs and clamour roar
Upon his death?

Macbeth.   I am settled, and bend up
Each corporal agent to this terrible feat.   80
Away, and mock the time with fairest show:
False face must hide what the false heart doth know.

                    [*they return to the chamber*

[2. 1.] *The same, one or two hours later. 'Enter' from
the back 'BANQUO, and FLEANCE with a torch before him'.
They come forward, leaving the door open behind them*

Banquo. How goes the night, boy?
Fleance [*gazing at the sky*]. The moon is down;
    I have not heard the clock.
Banquo. And she goes down at twelve.
Fleance.   I take't, 'tis later, sir.
Banquo. Hold, take my sword....There's husbandry
    in heaven,
Their candles are all out....

                    [*unclasps his belt with its dagger*
                    Take thee that too.
A heavy summons lies like lead upon me,

And yet I would not sleep. Merciful powers,
Restrain in me the cursèd thoughts that nature
Gives way to in repose! [*he starts*] Give me my sword,

'*Enter*' (*from the right*) '*MACBETH, and a servant,
with a torch*'

10 Who's there?

Macbeth. A friend.

Banquo. What, sir, not yet at rest? The king's a-bed.
He hath been in unusual pleasure, and
Sent forth great largess to your offices.
This diamond he greets your wife withal,
By the name of most kind hostess; and shut up
In measureless content.

Macbeth.   Being unprepared,
Our will became the servant to defect,
Which else should free have wrought.

Banquo.   All's well.
20 I dreamt last night of the three Weird Sisters:
To you they have showed some truth.

Macbeth.   I think not of them:
Yet, when we can entreat an hour to serve,
We would spend it in some words upon that business,
If you would grant the time.

Banquo.   At your kind'st leisure.

Macbeth. If you shall cleave to my consent, when 'tis,
It shall make honour for you.

Banquo.   So I lose none
In seeking to augment it, but still keep
My bosom franchised and allegiance clear,
I shall be counselled.

Macbeth.   Good repose the while!
30 *Banquo.* Thanks, sir: the like to you!

[*Banquo and Fleance go to their chamber*

Macbeth. Go bid thy mistress, when my drink is ready,
She strike upon the bell. Get thee to bed.
                    [*the servant goes; he sits at the table*
Is this a dagger which I see before me,
The handle toward my hand? Come, let me clutch thee:
I have thee not, and yet I see thee still.
Art thou not, fatal vision, sensible
To feeling as to sight? or art thou but
A dagger of the mind, a false creation,
Proceeding from the heat-oppresséd brain?
I see thee yet, in form as palpable   40
As this which now I draw.
Thou marshall'st me the way that I was going,
And such an instrument I was to use!   [*he rises*
Mine eyes are made the fools o'th'other senses,
Or else worth all the rest: I see thee still;
And on thy blade and dudgeon gouts of blood,
Which was not so before. There's no such thing:
It is the bloody business which informs
Thus to mine eyes....Now o'er the one half-world
Nature seems dead, and wicked dreams abuse   50
The curtained sleep; Witchcraft celebrates
Pale Hecate's off'rings; and withered Murder,
Alarumed by his sentinel, the wolf,
Whose howl's his watch, thus with his stealthy pace,
With Tarquin's ravishing strides, towards his design
Moves like a ghost. Thou sure and firm-set earth,
Hear not my steps, which way they walk, for fear
Thy very stones prate of my whereabout,
And take the present horror from the time,
Which now suits with it. Whiles I threat, he lives: 60
Words to the heat of deeds too cold breath gives.
                            [*'a bell rings'*
I go, and it is done: the bell invites me.

Hear it not, Duncan, for it is a knell
That summons thee to heaven, or to hell.

> [*he steals out by the open door at back, and
>   step by step climbs the stair. A pause*

[2. 2.]   LADY MACBETH *enters from the right,
                with a cup in her hand*

Lady M. That which hath made them drunk hath
    made me bold:
What hath quenched them hath given me fire. [*she
    pauses*] Hark! Peace:
It was the owl that shrieked, the fatal bellman,
Which gives the stern'st good-night. He is about it:
The doors are open; and the surfeited grooms
Do mock their charge with snores: I have drugged
    their possets,
That death and nature do contend about them,
Whether they live or die.
    Macbeth [*within*].   Who's there? what, ho!
    Lady M. Alack! I am afraid they have awaked,
10 And 'tis not done: th'attempt and not the deed
Confounds us. Hark! I laid their daggers ready,
He could not miss 'em. Had he not resembled
My father as he slept, I had done't.

> *She turns as if making towards the stair, to find
> MACBETH standing in the door, his arms bathed
> in blood and with two daggers clasped in his left
> hand. He totters forward*

                                My husband!
    Macbeth [*whispers*]. I have done the deed....Didst
        thou not hear a noise?
    Lady M. I heard the owl scream, and the crickets cry.
Did not you speak?
    Macbeth.   When?

Lady M.   Now.
Macbeth.   As I descended?
Lady M. Ay.
Macbeth. Hark!   [*they listen*
Who lies i'th' second chamber?
Lady M.   Donalbain.
Macbeth. This is a sorry sight.   20
                    [*stretching forth his right hand*
Lady M. A foolish thought, to say a sorry sight.   ●
Macbeth. There's one did laugh in's sleep, and one
    cried 'Murder!'
That they did wake each other: I stood and heard them:
But they did say their prayers, and addressed them
Again to sleep.
Lady M.   There are two lodged together.
Macbeth. One cried 'God bless us!' and 'Amen' the
    other,
As they had seen me with these hangman's hands:
List'ning their fear, I could not say 'Amen',
When they did say 'God bless us'.
Lady M. Consider it not so deeply.   30
Macbeth. But wherefore could not I pronounce
    'Amen'?
I had most need of blessing, and 'Amen'
Stuck in my throat.
Lady M.   These deeds must not be thought
After these ways; so, it will make us mad.
Macbeth. Methought I heard a voice cry 'Sleep no
    more!
Macbeth does murder sleep'—the innocent sleep,
Sleep that knits up the ravelled sleave of care,
The death of each day's life, sore labour's bath,
Balm of hurt minds, great Nature's second course,
Chief nourisher in life's feast,—   40

Lady M.   What do you mean?

Macbeth. Still it cried 'Sleep no more!' to all the
  house:
'Glamis hath murdered sleep, and therefore Cawdor
Shall sleep no more: Macbeth shall sleep no more!'

Lady M. Who was it that thus cried? Why, worthy
  thane,
You do unbend your noble strength, to think
So brainsickly of things. Go get some water,
And wash this filthy witness from your hand.
Why did you bring these daggers from the place?
They must lie there: go carry them, and smear
50 The sleepy grooms with blood.

Macbeth.   I'll go no more:
I am afraid to think what I have done;
Look on't again I dare not.

Lady M.   Infirm of purpose!
Give me the daggers: the sleeping and the dead
Are but as pictures: 'tis the eye of childhood
That fears a painted devil. If he do bleed,
I'll gild the faces of the grooms withal,
For it must seem their guilt.

                    [*she goes up. A knocking heard*

Macbeth.   Whence is that knocking?
How is't with me, when every noise appals me?
What hands are here? ha! they pluck out mine eyes!
60 Will all great Neptune's ocean wash this blood
Clean from my hand? No; this my hand will rather
The multitudinous seas incarnadine,
Making the green—one red.

          Lady Macbeth returns, closing the inner door

Lady M. My hands are of your colour; but I shame
To wear a heart so white. [*knocking*] I hear a knocking

At the south entry: retire we to our chamber:
A little water clears us of this deed:
How easy is it then! Your constancy
Hath left you unattended. [*knocking*] Hark! more
    knocking.
Get on your nightgown, lest occasion call us   70
And show us to be watchers: be not lost
So poorly in your thoughts.
   Macbeth. To know my deed, 'twere best not know
    myself.   [*knocking*
Wake Duncan with thy knocking! I would thou
    couldst!   [*they go in*

[2. 3.] *The knocking grows yet louder; a drunken*
           Porter enters the court

   Porter. Here's a knocking indeed! If a man were
porter of hell-gate, he should have old turning the key.
[*knocking*] Knock, knock, knock! Who's there, i'th'
name of Beelzebub? Here's a farmer, that hanged himself on th'expectation of plenty: come in, time-server;
have napkins enow about you, here you'll sweat for't.
[*knocking*] Knock, knock! Who's there, in th'other
devil's name? Faith, here's an equivocator, that could
swear in both the scales against either scale, who com-
mitted treason enough for God's sake, yet could not 10
equivocate to heaven: O, come in, equivocator. [*knocking*] Knock, knock, knock! Who's there? Faith, here's
an English tailor come hither, for stealing out of a French
hose: come in, tailor, here you may roast your goose.
[*knocking*] Knock, knock! never at quiet! What are you?
But this place is too cold for hell. I'll devil-porter it no
further: I had thought to have let in some of all pro-
fessions, that go the primrose way to th'everlasting

bonfire. [*knocking*] Anon, anon! I pray you, remember
20 the porter.   [*opens the gate*

'*Enter* MACDUFF *and* LENNOX'

Macduff. Was it so late, friend, ere you went to bed,
That you do lie so late?

Porter. Faith, sir, we were carousing till the second
cock: and drink, sir, is a great provoker of three things.

Macduff. What three things does drink especially
provoke?

Porter. Marry, sir, nose-painting, sleep, and urine.
Lechery, sir, it provokes and unprovokes: it provokes
the desire, but it takes away the performance. Therefore,
30 much drink may be said to be an equivocator with
lechery: it makes him, and it mars him; it sets him on,
and it takes him off; it persuades him, and disheartens
him; makes him stand to, and not stand to: in con-
clusion, equivocates him in a sleep, and giving him the
lie, leaves him.

Macduff. I believe drink gave thee the lie last night.

Porter. That it did, sir, i'the very throat on me: but
I requited him for his lie, and, I think, being too strong
for him, though he took up my legs sometime, yet I
40 made a shift to cast him.

Macduff. Is thy master stirring?

MACBETH *returns, in a dressing gown*

Our knocking has awaked him; here he comes.

Lennox. Good-morrow, noble sir.

Macbeth.   Good-morrow, both.

Macduff. Is the king stirring, worthy thane?

Macbeth.   Not yet.

Macduff. He did command me to call timely on him;
I have almost slipped the hour.

Macbeth.   I'll bring you to him.
                    [*they move towards the inner door*

Macduff. I know this is a joyful trouble to you;
But yet 'tis one.

Macbeth. The labour we delight in physics pain.
This is the door.   [*he points*

Macduff.   I'll make so bold to call,   30
For 'tis my limited service.   [*he goes in*

Lennox. Goes the king hence to-day?

Macbeth. He does: he did appoint so.

Lennox. The night has been unruly: where we lay,
Our chimneys were blown down, and, as they say,
Lamentings heard i'th'air, strange screams of death,
And prophesying with accents terrible
Of dire combustion and confused events
New hatched to th' woeful time. The obscure bird
Clamoured the livelong night: some say, the earth   60
Was feverous and did shake.

Macbeth.   'Twas a rough night.

Lennox. My young remembrance cannot parallel
A fellow to it.

MACDUFF *returns*

Macduff. O horror! horror! horror! Tongue, nor
    heart,
Cannot conceive nor name thee!

Macbeth, Lennox.   What's the matter?

Macduff. Confusion now hath made his master-
    piece!
Most sacrilegious murder hath broke ope
The Lord's anointed temple, and stole thence
The life o'th' building.

Macbeth.   What is't you say? the life?

Lennox. Mean you his majesty?   70

Macduff. Approach the chamber, and destroy your
   sight
With a new Gorgon: do not bid me speak;
See, and then speak yourselves.

       [*Macbeth and Lennox go up*
        Awake! awake!
Ring the alarum bell! Murder and treason!
Banquo and Donalbain! Malcolm, awake!
Shake off this downy sleep, death's counterfeit,
And look on death itself! up, up, and see
The great doom's image! Malcolm! Banquo!
As from your graves rise up, and walk like sprites,
80 To countenance this horror!   ['*bell rings*'

   '*Enter* LADY' MACBETH *in a dressing gown*

 Lady M.   What's the business,
That such a hideous trumpet calls to parley
The sleepers of the house? speak, speak!
 Macduff.   O, gentle lady,
'Tis not for you to hear what I can speak:
The repetition, in a woman's ear,
Would murder as it fell.

   '*Enter* BANQUO' *half-clad*

     O Banquo! Banquo!
Our royal master's murdered!
 Lady M.   Woe, alas!
What, in our house?
 Banquo.   Too cruel, any where.
Dear Duff, I prithee, contradict thyself,
And say it is not so.

   MACBETH *and* LENNOX *return*

90 *Macbeth.* Had I but died an hour before this chance,

I had lived a blesséd time; for from this instant
There's nothing serious in mortality:
All is but toys: renown and grace is dead,
The wine of life is drawn, and the mere lees
Is left this vault to brag of.

*MALCOLM and DONALBAIN come in haste through
the door on the right*

Donalbain. What is amiss?
  Macbeth.   You are, and do not know't:
The spring, the head, the fountain of your blood
Is stopped—the very source of it is stopped.
  Macduff. Your royal father's murdered.
  Malcolm.   O, by whom?
  Lennox. Those of his chamber, as it seemed, had   100
      done't:
Their hands and faces were all badged with blood,
So were their daggers, which unwiped we found
Upon their pillows:
They stared and were distracted, no man's life
Was to be trusted with them.
  Macbeth. O, yet I do repent me of my fury,
That I did kill them.
  Macduff.   Wherefore did you so?
  Macbeth. Who can be wise, amazed, temp'rate and
      furious,
Loyal and neutral, in a moment? no man:
Th'expedition of my violent love   110
Outrun the pauser, reason. Here lay Duncan,
His silver skin laced with his golden blood,
And his gashed stabs looked like a breach in nature
For ruin's wasteful entrance: there, the murderers,
Steeped in the colours of their trade, their daggers
Unmannerly breeched with gore: who could refrain,

That had a heart to love, and in that heart
Courage to make's love known?
    Lady M. [*seeming to faint*]   Help me hence, ho!

            MACBETH goes to her

    Macduff. Look to the lady.
    (*Malcolm.*   Why do we hold our tongues,
120 That most may claim this argument for ours?
    (*Donalbain.* What should be spoken here, where our
        fate,
Hid in an auger-hole, may rush and seize us?
Let's away.
Our tears are not yet brewed.
    (*Malcolm.*   Nor our strong sorrow
Upon the foot of motion.   [*enter waiting-women*
    Banquo [*directs them*].   Look to the lady...
                [*they lead her forth*
And when we have our naked frailties hid,
That suffer in exposure, let us meet,
And question this most bloody piece of work,
To know it further. Fears and scruples shake us:
130 In the great hand of God I stand, and thence
Against the undivulged pretence I fight
Of treasonous malice.
    Macduff.   And so do I.
    All.   So all.
    Macbeth. Let's briefly put on manly readiness.
And meet i'th'hall together.
    All.   Well contented.
          [*all go in but Malcolm and Donalbain*
    Malcolm. What will you do? Let's not consort with
    them:
To show an unfelt sorrow is an office
Which the false man does easy. I'll to England.

Donalbain. To Ireland, I: our separated fortune
Shall keep us both the safer: where we are
There's daggers in men's smiles: the near in blood,　　140
The nearer bloody.

Malcolm.　　　　　This murderous shaft that's shot
Hath not yet lighted, and our safest way
Is to avoid the aim. Therefore to horse,
And let us not be dainty of leave-taking,
But shift away: there's warrant in that theft
Which steals itself when there's no mercy left.

[they go

[2. 4.]　　　*Before Macbeth's castle. A day
strangely dark*

'*Enter Ross with an Old Man*'

Old Man. Threescore and ten I can remember well,
Within the volume of which time I have seen
Hours dreadful and things strange; but this sore night
Hath trifled former knowings.

Ross. [looks up]　　　　　Ha, good father,
Thou seest the heavens, as troubled with man's act,
Threatens his bloody stage: by th' clock 'tis day,
And yet dark night strangles the travelling lamp:
Is't night's predominance, or the day's shame,
That darkness does the face of earth entomb,
When living light should kiss it?

Old Man.　　　　　　　'Tis unnatural,　　10
Even like the deed that's done. On Tuesday last
A falcon towering in her pride of place
Was by a mousing owl hawked at and killed.

Ross. And Duncan's horses—a thing most strange and
certain—
Beauteous and swift, the minions of their race,

Turned wild in nature, broke their stalls, flung out,
Contending 'gainst obedience, as they would make
War with mankind.

    Old Man.   'Tis said they eat each other.

    Ross. They did so, to th'amazement of mine eyes,
20 That looked upon't.

        MACDUFF comes from the castle

                   Here comes the good Macduff.
How goes the world, sir, now?

    Macduff [*points at the sky*].   Why, see you not?

    Ross. Is't known who did this more than bloody
      deed?

    Macduff. Those that Macbeth hath slain.

    Ross.   Alas, the day!
What good could they pretend?

    Macduff.   They were suborned.
Malcolm and Donalbain, the king's two sons,
Are stol'n away and fled, which puts upon them
Suspicion of the deed.

    Ross.   'Gainst nature still!
Thriftless ambition, that wilt ravin up
Thine own life's means! Then 'tis most like
30 The sovereignty will fall upon Macbeth.

    Macduff. He is already named, and gone to Scone
To be invested.

    Ross.   Where is Duncan's body?

    Macduff. Carried to Colme kill,
The sacred storehouse of his predecessors,
And guardian of their bones.

    Ross.   Will you to Scone?

    Macduff. No cousin, I'll to Fife.

                      Well, I will thither.

Macduff. Well, may you see things well done there:
   adieu!
Lest our old robes sit easier than our new!
  Ross. Farewell, father.
  Old Man. God's benison go with you, and with those 40
That would make good of bad and friends of foes!

                             [*they go*

        [*Some weeks pass*]

[3. 1.]   *An audience chamber in the palace at*
                    Forres

           BANQUO enters

  Banquo. Thou hast it now, King, Cawdor, Glamis, all,
As the weïrd women promised, and I fear
Thou play'dst most foully for't: yet it was said
It should not stand in thy posterity,
But that myself should be the root and father
Of many kings. If there come truth from them—
As upon thee, Macbeth, their speeches shine—
Why, by the verities on thee made good,
May they not be my oracles as well,
And set me up in hope? But hush, no more.   10

'*Sennet sounded. Enter* MACBETH, *as King,* LADY'
MACBETH, *as Queen,* 'LENNOX, ROSS, *Lords, and*
attendants'

  Macbeth. Here's our chief guest.
  Lady M.   If he had been forgotten,
It had been as a gap in our great feast,
And all-thing unbecoming.
  Macbeth. To-night we hold a solemn supper, sir,
And I'll request your presence.

  Banquo.   Let your highness
Command upon me, to the which my duties
Are with a most indissoluble tie
For ever knit.
  Macbeth. Ride you this afternoon?
  Banquo.   Ay, my good lord.
20 *Macbeth.* We should have else desired your good advice
(Which still hath been both grave and prosperous)
In this day's council; but we'll take to-morrow.
Is't far you ride?
  Banquo. As far, my lord, as will fill up the time
'Twixt this and supper. Go not my horse the better,
I must become a borrower of the night
For a dark hour or twain.
  Macbeth.   Fail not our feast.
  Banquo. My lord, I will not.
  Macbeth. We hear our bloody cousins are bestowed
30 In England and in Ireland, not confessing
Their cruel parricide, filling their hearers
With strange invention: but of that to-morrow,
When therewithal we shall have cause of state
Craving us jointly. Hie you to horse: adieu,
Till you return at night. Goes Fleance with you?
  Banquo. Ay, my good lord: our time does call upon's.
  Macbeth. I wish your horses swift and sure of foot;
And so I do commend you to their backs.
Farewell.   *[Banquo goes*
40 Let every man be master of his time
Till seven at night; to make society
The sweeter welcome, we will keep ourself
Till supper-time alone: while then, God be with you!
      [all depart but Macbeth and a servant
Sirrah, a word with you: attend those men
Our pleasure?

Attendant. They are, my lord, without the palace gate.
Macbeth. Bring them before us.   [*the servant goes*
                To be thus is nothing,
But to be safely thus: our fears in Banquo
Stick deep, and in his royalty of nature
Reigns that which would be feared. 'Tis much he dares, 50
And, to that dauntless temper of his mind,
He hath a wisdom that doth guide his valour
To act in safety. There is none but he
Whose being I do fear: and under him
My Genius is rebuked, as it is said
Mark Antony's was by Cæsar. He chid the Sisters,
When first they put the name of king upon me,
And bade them speak to him; then prophet-like
They hailed him father to a line of kings:
Upon my head they placed a fruitless crown,   60
And put a barren sceptre in my gripe,
Thence to be wrenched with an unlineal hand,
No son of mine succeeding. If't be so,
For Banquo's issue have I filed my mind,
For them the gracious Duncan have I murdered,
Put rancours in the vessel of my peace
Only for them, and mine eternal jewel
Given to the common enemy of man,
To make them kings, the seed of Banquo kings!
Rather than so, come Fate into the list,   70
And champion me to th'utterance. Who's there?

     The servant returns 'with two murderers'

Now go to the door, and stay there till we call.
                       [*servant goes out*
Was it not yesterday we spoke together?
   1 *Murderer.* It was, so please your highness.
   Macbeth.   Well then, now

Have you considered of my speeches? Know
That it was he in the times past which held you
So under fortune, which you thought had been
Our innocent self: this I made good to you
In our last conference; passed in probation with you,
80 How you were borne in hand, how crossed, the
            instruments,
Who wrought with them, and all things else that might
To half a soul and to a notion crazed
Say 'Thus did Banquo'.
  1 *Murderer*.   You made it known to us.
  Macbeth. I did so; and went further, which is now
Our point of second meeting. Do you find
Your patience so predominant in your nature,
That you can let this go? Are you so gospelled,
To pray for this good man, and for his issue,
Whose heavy hand hath bowed you to the grave
90 And beggared yours for ever?
  1 *Murderer*.   We are men, my liege.
  Macbeth. Ay, in the catalogue ye go for men,
As hounds and greyhounds, mongrels, spaniels, curs,
Shoughs, water-rugs, and demi-wolves, are clept
All by the name of dogs: the valued file
Distinguishes the swift, the slow, the subtle,
The housekeeper, the hunter, every one
According to the gift which bounteous nature
Hath in him closed, whereby he does receive
Particular addition, from the bill
100 That writes them all alike: and so of men.
Now, if you have a station in the file,
Not i'th' worst rank of manhood, say't,
And I will put that business in your bosoms,
Whose execution takes your enemy off,
Grapples you to the heart and love of us,

Who wear our health but sickly in his life,
Which in his death were perfect.

  2 Murderer.   I am one, my liege,
Whom the vile blows and buffets of the world
Hath so incensed that I am reckless what
I do to spite the world.

  1 Murderer.   And I another   110
So weary with disasters, tugged with fortune,
That I would set my life on any chance,
To mend it, or be rid on't.

  Macbeth.   Both of you
Know Banquo was your enemy.

  Both Murderers.   True, my lord.

  Macbeth. So is he mine: and in such bloody distance,
That every minute of his being thrusts
Against my near'st of life: and though I could
With barefaced power sweep him from my sight,
And bid my will avouch it, yet I must not,
For certain friends that are both his and mine,   120
Whose loves I may not drop, but wail his fall
Who I myself struck down: and thence it is
That I to your assistance do make love,
Masking the business from the common eye,
For sundry weighty reasons.

  2 Murderer.   We shall, my lord,
Perform what you command us.

  1 Murderer.   Though our lives—

  Macbeth. Your spirits shine through you. Within this
    hour at most
I will advise you where to plant yourselves,
Acquaint you with the perfect spy o'th' time,
The moment on't, for't must be done to-night,   130
And something from the palace; always thought
That I require a clearness: and with him—

To leave no rubs nor botches in the work—
Fleance his son, that keeps him company,
Whose absence is no less material to me
Than is his father's, must embrace the fate
Of that dark hour. Resolve yourselves apart;
I'll come to you anon.
   Both Murderers.   We are resolved, my lord.
   Macbeth. I'll call upon you straight; abide within.
                                  [they go
140 It is concluded: Banquo, thy soul's flight,
If it find heaven, must find it out to-night.
                        [he leaves by another door

[3. 2.]   *LADY MACBETH enters with a servant*

   Lady M. Is Banquo gone from court?
   Servant. Ay, madam, but returns again to-night.
   Lady M. Say to the king, I would attend his leisure
For a few words.
   Servant.   Madam, I will.   *[he goes*
   Lady M.   Nought's had, all's spent,
Where our desire is got without content:
'Tis safer to be that which we destroy
Than by destruction dwell in doubtful joy.

        MACBETH enters lost in thought

How now, my lord! why do you keep alone,
Of sorriest fancies your companions making,
10 Using those thoughts which should indeed have died
With them they think on? Things without all remedy
Should be without regard: what's done, is done.
   Macbeth. We have scorched the snake, not killed it:
She'll close and be herself, whilst our poor malice
Remains in danger of her former tooth.

But let the frame of things disjoint, both the worlds
    suffer,
Ere we will eat our meal in fear, and sleep
In the affliction of these terrible dreams
That shake us nightly: better be with the dead,
Whom we, to gain our peace, have sent to peace,   20
Than on the torture of the mind to lie
In restless ecstasy. Duncan is in his grave;
After life's fitful fever he sleeps well;
Treason has done his worst: nor steel, nor poison,
Malice domestic, foreign levy, nothing,
Can touch him further.
    Lady M.   Come on;
Gentle my lord, sleek o'er your rugged looks,
Be bright and jovial among your guests to-night.
    Macbeth. So shall I, love, and so I pray be you:
Let your remembrance apply to Banquo;   30
Present him eminence, both with eye and tongue:
Unsafe the while, that we
Must lave our honours in these flattering streams,
And make our faces vizards to our hearts,
Disguising what they are.
    Lady M.   You must leave this.
    Macbeth. O, full of scorpions is my mind, dear
    wife!
Thou know'st that Banquo and his Fleance lives.
    Lady M. But in them nature's copy's not eterne.
    Macbeth. There's comfort yet, they are assailable,
Then be thou jocund: ere the bat hath flown   40
His cloistered flight, ere to black Hecate's summons
The shard-borne beetle with his drowsy hums
Hath rung night's yawning peal, there shall be done
A deed of dreadful note.
    Lady M.   What's to be done?

Macbeth. Be innocent of the knowledge, dearest chuck,
Till thou applaud the deed...Come, seeling night,
Scarf up the tender eye of pitiful day,
And with thy bloody and invisible hand
Cancel and tear to pieces that great bond
50 †Which keeps me paled! Light thickens, and the crow
Makes wing to th' rooky wood:
Good things of day begin to droop and drowse,
Whiles night's black agents to their preys do rouse.
Thou marvell'st at my words: but hold thee still;
Things bad begun make strong themselves by ill:
So, prithee, go with me.   [*they go*

[3. 3.] *A steep lane leading through a wood to gates of
the royal park, some way from the palace. The two
murderers come up, with a third*

1 *Murderer.* But who did bid thee join with us?
3 *Murderer.*   Macbeth.
2 *Murderer.* He needs not our mistrust, since he
    delivers
Our offices and what we have to do,
To the direction just.
    1 *Murderer.*   Then stand with us.
The west yet glimmers with some streaks of day:
Now spurs the lated traveller apace
To gain the timely inn, and near approaches
The subject of our watch.
    3 *Murderer.*   Hark! I hear horses.
    Banquo [*at a distance*] Give us a light there, ho!
    2 *Murderer.*   Then 'tis he; the rest
10 That are within the note of expectation
Already are i'th' court.
    1 *Murderer.*   His horses go about.

3 *Murderer*. Almost a mile: but he does usually—
So all men do—from hence to th' palace gate
Make it their walk.

  'BANQUO *and* FLEANCE *with a torch' are seen
     coming up the lane*

2 *Murderer*.   A light, a light!
3 *Murderer*.   'Tis he.
1 *Murderer*. Stand to't.
Banquo. It will be rain to-night.
1 *Murderer*.   Let it come down.
    [1 *Murderer strikes out the torch; the
        others set upon Banquo*
Banquo. O, treachery! Fly, good Fleance, fly, fly, fly!
Thou mayst revenge. O slave!
       [*he dies; Fleance escapes*
3 *Murderer*. Who did strike out the light?
1 *Murderer*.   Was't not the way?
3 *Murderer*. There's but one down; the son is fled.
2 *Murderer*.   We have lost 20
Best half of our affair.
1 *Murderer*. Well, let's away, and say how much is
  done.   [*they go*

[3. 4.] *The hall of the palace. At the upper end a dais
with doors to left and right, between which are two thrones
and a table before them, while a longer table, at right
angles, extends down the room*

 A 'banquet prepared. *Enter* MACBETH, LADY' MAC-
BETH, 'ROSS, LENNOX, Lords, and attendants'

 Macbeth. You know your own degrees, sit down: at
  first
And last, the hearty welcome.

Lords.   Thanks to your majesty.

*Macbeth leads Lady Macbeth to the dais; the Lords
sit on either side of the long table, leaving an empty stool
at the head*

Macbeth. Ourself will mingle with society,
And play the humble host:
                    [*Lady Macbeth ascends to her throne*
Our hostess keeps her state, but in best time
We will require her welcome.
    Lady M. Pronounce it for me, sir, to all our friends,
For my heart speaks they are welcome.

As Macbeth passes by the door on the left 1 *Murderer
appears thereat. The Lords rise and bow to Lady
Macbeth*

    Macbeth. See, they encounter thee with their hearts'
        thanks.
10 Both sides are even: here I'll sit i'th' midst.
                        [*points to the empty stool*
Be large in mirth, anon we'll drink a measure
The table round.
    [*turns to the door*] There's blood upon thy face.
    (*Murderer.* 'Tis Banquo's then.
    (*Macbeth.* 'Tis better thee without than he within.
Is he dispatched?
    (*Murderer.* My lord, his throat is cut, that I did for
        him.
    (*Macbeth.* Thou art the best o'th' cut-throats! Yet
        he's good
That did the like for Fleance: if thou didst it,
Thou art the nonpareil.
    (*Murderer.*   Most royal sir,
20 Fleance is 'scaped.

(*Macbeth.* Then comes my fit again: I had else been
    perfect;
Whole as the marble, founded as the rock,
As broad and general as the casing air:
But now I am cabined, cribbed, confined, bound in
To saucy doubts and fears. But Banquo's safe?
  (*Murderer.* Ay, my good lord: safe in a ditch he
    bides,
With twenty trenchèd gashes on his head;
The least a death to nature.
  (*Macbeth.*   Thanks for that:
There the grown serpent lies; the worm that's fled
Hath nature that in time will venom breed,   30
No teeth for th' present. Get thee gone; to-morrow
We'll hear ourselves again.   [*murderer goes*
   Lady M.   My royal lord,
You do not give the cheer. The feast is sold
That is not often vouched, while 'tis a-making,
'Tis given with welcome: to feed were best at home;
From thence the sauce to meat is ceremony;
Meeting were bare without it.

        [*'The Ghost of Banquo' appears, 'and sits in
            Macbeth's place'*

   Macbeth.   Sweet remembrancer!
Now good digestion wait on appetite,
And health on both!
   Lennox.   May't please your highness sit.
   Macbeth. Here had we now our country's honour
    roofed,   40
Were the graced person of our Banquo present;
Who may I rather challenge for unkindness
Than pity for mischance!
   Ross.   His absence, sir,

Lays blame upon his promise. Please't your highness
To grace us with your royal company?

   Macbeth. The table's full.

   Lennox.   Here is a place reserved, sir.

   Macbeth. Where?

   Lennox. Here, my good lord....What is't that moves
      your highness?

   Macbeth. Which of you have done this?

   Lords.   What, my good lord?

50 *Macbeth.* Thou canst not say I did it: never shake
   Thy gory locks at me.   [*Lady Macbeth rises*

   Ross. Gentlemen, rise, his highness is not well.

   Lady M. [*coming down*] Sit, worthy friends: my lord
      is often thus,

And hath been from his youth: pray you, keep seat,
The fit is momentary, upon a thought
He will again be well: if much you note him,
You shall offend him and extend his passion:
Feed, and regard him not. [*aside*] Are you a man?

   (*Macbeth.* Ay, and a bold one, that dare look on that
60 Which might appal the devil.

   (*Lady M.*   O proper stuff!
This is the very painting of your fear:
This is the air-drawn dagger which, you said,
Led you to Duncan. O, these flaws and starts
(Impostors to true fear) would well become
A woman's story at a winter's fire,
Authorized by her grandam....Shame itself!
Why do you make such faces? When all's done,
You look but on a stool.

   (*Macbeth.* Prithee, see there! behold! look! lo! how
      say you?

70 Why what care I? If thou canst nod, speak too.
If charnel-houses and our graves must send

Those that we bury back, our monuments
Shall be the maws of kites.   [*the Ghost vanishes*
  (*Lady M.*   What! quite unmanned in folly?
  (*Macbeth.* If I stand here, I saw him.
  (*Lady M.*   Fie, for shame!
  (*Macbeth* [*paces to and fro*]. Blood hath been shed ere
      now, i'th'olden time,
Ere humane statute purged the gentle weal;
Ay, and since too, murders have been performed
Too terrible for the ear: the time has been,
That, when the brains were out, the man would die,
And there an end: but now they rise again,   80
With twenty mortal murders on their crowns,
And push us from our stools....This is more strange
Than such a murder is.
  Lady M. [*touches his arm*] My worthy lord,
Your noble friends do lack you.
  Macbeth.   I do forget...
Do not muse at me, my most worthy friends;
I have a strange infirmity, which is nothing
To those that know me. Come, love and health to all;
Then I'll sit down. Give me some wine, fill full.

          [*as he raises his cup, the Ghost reappears
              in the seat behind him*

I drink to th' general joy o'th' whole table,
And to our dear friend Banquo, whom we miss;   90
Would he were here! to all, and him we thirst,
And all to all!
  Lords [*drinking*]. Our duties, and the pledge.
  Macbeth [*turns to his seat*]. Avaunt! and quit my sight!
      let the earth hide thee!
          [*drops the cup*]
Thy bones are marrowless, thy blood is cold;

Thou hast no speculation in those eyes
Which thou dost glare with!

    Lady M.   Think of this, good peers,
But as a thing of custom: 'tis no other;
Only it spoils the pleasure of the time.

    Macbeth. What man dare, I dare:
100 Approach thou like the ruggéd Russian bear,
The armed rhinoceros, or th'Hyrcan tiger,
Take any shape but that, and my firm nerves
Shall never tremble: or be alive again,
And dare me to the desert with thy sword;
If trembling I inhabit then, protest me
The baby of a girl. Hence, horrible shadow!
Unreal mock'ry, hence!   [*the Ghost vanishes*
                    Why, so; being gone,
I am a man again. Pray you, sit still.

    Lady M. You have displaced the mirth, broke the
        good meeting,
110 With most admired disorder.

    Macbeth.   Can such things be,
And overcome us like a summer's cloud,
Without our special wonder? You make me strange
Even to the disposition that I owe,
When now I think you can behold such sights,
And keep the natural ruby of your cheeks,
When mine is blanched with fear.

    Ross.   What sights, my lord?

    Lady M. I pray you, speak not; he grows worse and
        worse;
Question enrages him: at once, good night.
Stand not upon the order of your going,   [*they rise*
120 But go at once.

    Lennox.   Good night, and better health
Attend his majesty!

Lady M.   A kind good night to all!

                                        [*they leave*

Macbeth. It will have blood; they say, blood will
     have blood:
Stones have been known to move and trees to speak;
Augures and understood relations have
By maggot-pies and choughs and rooks brought forth
The secret'st man of blood....What is the night?

  Lady M. Almost at odds with morning, which is
     which.

  Macbeth. How say'st thou, that Macduff denies his
     person
At our great bidding?

  Lady M.   Did you send to him, sir?

  Macbeth. I hear it by the way; but I will send: 130
There's not a one of them but in his house
I keep a servant fee'd....I will to-morrow
(And betimes I will) to the Weïrd Sisters:
More shall they speak; for now I am bent to know,
By the worst means, the worst. For mine own good
All causes shall give way: I am in blood
Stepped in so far that, should I wade no more,
Returning were as tedious as go o'er:
Strange things I have in head that will to hand,
Which must be acted ere they may be scanned.   140

  Lady M. You lack the season of all natures, sleep.

  Macbeth. Come, we'll to sleep. My strange and
     self-abuse
Is the initiate fear that wants hard use:
We are yet but young in deed.   [*they go*

⌜3. 5.   *A heath*   ⌝

'*Thunder. Enter the three Witches*',
meeting HECATE

1 *Witch.* Why, how now, Hecat, you look angerly.
  Hecate. Have I not reason, beldams as you are,
Saucy and overbold? How did you dare
To trade and traffic with Macbeth
In riddles and affairs of death;
And I, the mistress of your charms,
The close contriver of all harms,
Was never called to bear my part,
Or show the glory of our art?
10 And, which is worse, all you have done
Hath been but for a wayward son,
Spiteful and wrathful, who (as others do)
Loves for his own ends, not for you.
But make amends now: get you gone,
And at the pit of Acheron
Meet me i'th' morning: thither he
Will come to know his destiny.
Your vessels and your spells provide,
Your charms and every thing beside.
20 I am for th'air; this night I'll spend
Unto a dismal and a fatal end.
Great business must be wrought ere noon:
Upon the corner of the moon
There hangs a vap'rous drop profound;
I'll catch it ere it come to ground:
And that distilled by magic sleights
Shall raise such artificial sprites
As by the strength of their illusion
Shall draw him on to his confusion.

He shall spurn fate, scorn death, and bear   30
His hopes 'bove wisdom, grace, and fear:
And you all know security
Is mortals' chiefest enemy.

> *'Music and a song': 'Come away, come away,' &c.*
>   *A cloud descends*

Hark, I am called: my little spirit, see,
Sits in a foggy cloud, and stays for me.
> [*she flies away on the cloud*

1 *Witch.* Come, let's make haste; she'll soon be back
     again.   *They vanish*   ]

[3. 6.]   *A castle in Scotland*

'Enter LENNOX *and another Lord*'

Lennox. My former speeches have but hit your
     thoughts,
Which can interpret farther: only I say
Things have been strangely borne. The gracious
     Duncan
Was pitied of Macbeth: marry, he was dead:
And the right valiant Banquo walked too late—
Whom you may say (if't please you) Fleance killed,
For Fleance fled: men must not walk too late.
Who cannot want the thought, how monstrous
It was for Malcolm and for Donalbain
To kill their gracious father? damnéd fact!   10
How it did grieve Macbeth! did he not straight,
In pious rage, the two delinquents tear,
That were the slaves of drink and thralls of sleep?
Was not that nobly done? Ay, and wisely too;
For 'twould have angered any heart alive

To hear the men deny't. So that, I say,
He has borne all things well: and I do think
That, had he Duncan's sons under his key
(As, an't please heaven, he shall not) they should find
20 What 'twere to kill a father; so should Fleance.
But, peace! for from broad words, and 'cause he failed
His presence at the tyrant's feast, I hear,
Macduff lives in disgrace. Sir, can you tell
Where he bestows himself?

    Lord.   The son of Duncan
(From whom this tyrant holds the due of birth)
Lives in the English court, and is received
Of the most pious Edward with such grace
That the malevolence of fortune nothing
Takes from his high respect. Thither Macduff
30 Is gone to pray the holy king, upon his aid
To wake Northumberland and warlike Siward,
That by the help of these (with Him above
To ratify the work) we may again
Give to our tables meat, sleep to our nights;
Free from our feasts and banquets bloody knives;
Do faithful homage and receive free honours:
All which we pine for now. And this report
Hath so exasperate the king that he
Prepares for some attempt of war.

    Lennox.   Sent he to Macduff?
40   *Lord.* He did: and with an absolute 'Sir, not I',
The cloudy messenger turns me his back,
And hums, as who should say, 'You'll rue the time
That clogs me with this answer'.

    Lennox.   And that well might
Advise him to a caution, t'hold what distance
His wisdom can provide. Some holy angel
Fly to the court of England and unfold

His message ere he come, that a swift blessing
May soon return to this our suffering country
Under a hand accursed!
 Lord.   I'll send my prayers with him.
              [they go

[4. 1.] *A cavern and in the midst a fiery pit with a boiling
cauldron above it. 'Thunder', as the Weird Sisters rise,
one after the other, from the flames*

 1 *Witch*. Thrice the brinded cat hath mewed.
 2 *Witch*. Thrice and once the hedge-pig whined.
 3 *Witch*. Harpier cries:— 'Tis time, 'tis time.
 1 *Witch*. Round about the cauldron go:
In the poisoned entrails throw.
       [they move leftwards about it
Toad, that under cold stone
Days and nights has thirty-one
Sweltered venom sleeping got,
Boil thou first i'th' charméd pot!
 All. Double, double toil and trouble;   10
Fire burn and cauldron bubble.
         [they stir the cauldron
 2 *Witch*. Fillet of a fenny snake,
In the cauldron boil and bake:
Eye of newt and toe of frog,
Wool of bat and tongue of dog,
Adder's fork and blind-worm's sting,
Lizard's leg and howlet's wing,
For a charm of powerful trouble,
Like a hell-broth boil and bubble.
 All. Double, double toil and trouble;   20
Fire burn and cauldron bubble.   *[they stir*

3 *Witch.* Scale of dragon, tooth of wolf,
Witch's mummy, maw and gulf
Of the ravined salt-sea shark,
Root of hemlock digged i'th' dark,
Liver of blaspheming Jew,
Gall of goat and slips of yew
Slivered in the moon's eclipse,
Nose of Turk and Tartar's lips,
30 Finger of birth-strangled babe
Ditch-delivered by a drab,
Make the gruel thick and slab:
Add thereto a tiger's chaudron,
For th'ingredience of our cauldron.
  All. Double, double toil and trouble;
Fire burn and cauldron bubble.   [*they stir*
  2 *Witch.* Cool it with a baboon's blood,
Then the charm is firm and good.

['*Enter* HECATE *and the other three Witches*'   ]

  Hecate. O, well done! I commend your pains,
40 And every one shall share i'th' gains:
          And now about the cauldron sing,
          Like elves and fairies in a ring,
          Enchanting all that you put in.

['*Music and a song: Black spirits, &c.*' *Hecate goes*]

  2 *Witch.* By the pricking of my thumbs,
Something wicked this way comes:
Open, locks,
Whoever knocks!

    A door flies open, showing MACBETH *without*

  Macbeth [*enters*]. How now, you secret, black, and
    midnight hags!
What is't you do?

All.   A deed without a name.

Macbeth. I conjure you, by that which you profess 50
(Howe'er you come to know it) answer me:
Though you untie the winds and let them fight
Against the churches; though the yesty waves
Confound and swallow navigation up;
Though bladed corn be lodged and trees blown
        down;
Though castles topple on their warders' heads;
Though palaces and pyramids do slope
Their heads to their foundations; though the treasure
Of Nature's germens tumble all together,
Even till destruction sicken; answer me   60
To what I ask you.

1 *Witch.*   Speak.
2 *Witch.*   Demand.
3 *Witch.*   We'll answer.
1 *Witch.* Say if th'hadst rather hear it from our
        mouths,
Or from our masters.

Macbeth.   Call 'em, let me see 'em!

1 *Witch.* Pour in sow's blood, that hath eaten
        Her nine farrow; grease that's sweaten
        From the murderer's gibbet throw
        Into the flame.

All.   Come, high or low;
        Thyself and office deftly show.

'*Thunder. First Apparition, an armed head*' *like
        Macbeth's, rises from the cauldron*

Macbeth. Tell me, thou unknown power—
1 *Witch.*   He knows thy thought:
Hear his speech, but say thou nought.   70

1 *Apparition.* Macbeth! Macbeth! Macbeth! beware
    Macduff,
Beware the thane of Fife. Dismiss me. Enough.

                     ['*descends*'

Macbeth. Whate'er thou art, for thy good caution
    thanks;
Thou hast harped my fear aright. But one word more—
1 *Witch.* He will not be commanded: here's another,
More potent than the first.

    '*Thunder. Second Apparition, a bloody child*'

2 *Apparition.* Macbeth! Macbeth! Macbeth!
Macbeth. Had I three ears, I'ld hear thee.
2 *Apparition.* Be bloody, bold, and resolute: laugh to
    scorn
80 The power of man; for none of woman born
    Shall harm Macbeth.   ['*descends*'
    Macbeth. Then live, Macduff: what need I fear of
        thee?
But yet I'll make assurance double sure,
And take a bond of fate: thou shalt not live,
That I may tell pale-hearted fear it lies,
And sleep in spite of thunder.

    '*Thunder. Third Apparition, a child crowned, with
             a tree in his hand*'

                        What is this,
That rises like the issue of a king,
And wears upon his baby-brow the round
And top of sovereignty?
    All.   Listen, but speak not to't.
90 3 *Apparition.* Be lion-mettled, proud, and take no care
    Who chafes, who frets, or where conspirers are:
    Macbeth shall never vanquished be until

Great Birnam wood to high Dunsinane hill
Shall come against him.   ['*descend*'
  Macbeth.   That will never be;
Who can impress the forest, bid the tree
Unfix his earth-bound root? Sweet bodements! good.
Rebellious dead, rise never, till the wood
Of Birnam rise, and our high-placed Macbeth
Shall live the lease of nature, pay his breath
To time and mortal custom. Yet my heart   100
Throbs to know one thing; tell me, if your art
Can tell so much: shall Banquo's issue ever
Reign in this kingdom?
  All.   Seek to know no more.
  Macbeth. I will be satisfied: deny me this,
And an eternal curse fall on you! Let me know....

        '*Hautboys*' *play as the cauldron descends*

Why sinks that cauldron? and what noise is this?
  1 *Witch.* Show!
  2 *Witch.* Show!
  3 *Witch.* Show!
  All. Show his eyes, and grieve his heart;   110
Come like shadows, so depart.

'*A show of eight kings*', *who pass one by one across the
back of the cavern as Macbeth speaks, the* '*last with a
glass in his hand*'; *Banquo's Ghost following*

  Macbeth. Thou art too like the spirit of Banquo:
      down!
Thy crown does sear mine eye-balls. And thy hair,
Thou other gold-bound brow, is like the first.
A third is like the former. Filthy hags!
Why do you show me this?—A fourth? Start, eyes!
What, will the line stretch out to th' crack of doom?

Another yet? A seventh? I'll see no more:
And yet the eighth appears, who bears a glass
120 Which shows me many more; and some I see
That two-fold balls and treble sceptres carry.
Horrible sight!...Now I see 'tis true,
For the blood-boltered Banquo smiles upon me,
And points at them for his. What, is this so?
[1 Witch. Ay, sir, all this is so. But why   ]
Stands Macbeth thus amazedly?
Come, sisters, cheer we up his sprites,
And show the best of our delights.
I'll charm the air to give a sound,
130 While you perform your antic round:
That this great king may kindly say
[Our duties did his welcome pay.]

'*Music. The Witches dance, and vanish*'

Macbeth. Where are they? Gone? Let this per-
nicious hour
Stand aye accursèd in the calendar
Come in, without there!

'*Enter* LENNOX'

Lennox.   What's your grace's will?
Macbeth. Saw you the Weïrd Sisters?
Lennox.   No, my lord.
Macbeth. Came they not by you?
Lennox.   No indeed, my lord.
Macbeth. Infected be the air whereon they ride,
And damned all those that trust them! I did hear
140 The galloping of horse. Who was't came by?
Lennox. 'Tis two or three, my lord, that bring you
word
Macduff is fled to England.

Macbeth.   Fled to England!

Lennox. Ay, my good lord.

(*Macbeth.* Time, thou anticipat'st my dread exploits:
The flighty purpose never is o'ertook
Unless the deed go with it. From this moment
The very firstlings of my heart shall be
The firstlings of my hand. And even now
To crown my thoughts with acts, be it thought and
      done:
The castle of Macduff I will surprise,   150
Seize upon Fife, give to th'edge o'th' sword
His wife, his babes, and all unfortunate souls
That trace him in his line. No boasting like a fool;
This deed I'll do before this purpose cool.
But no more sights! [*aloud*] Where are these gentlemen?
Come, bring me where they are.   [*they go*

[4. 2.]   *Fife. Macduff's castle*

'*Enter* Macduff's *Wife, her Son, and* Ross'

L. Macduff. What had he done, to make him fly the
      land?

Ross. You must have patience, madam.

L. Macduff.   He had none:
His flight was madness: when our actions do not,
Our fears do make us traitors.

Ross.   You know not
Whether it was his wisdom or his fear.

L. Macduff. Wisdom! to leave his wife, to leave his
      babes,
His mansion and his titles, in a place
From whence himself does fly? He loves us not;

He wants the natural touch: for the poor wren,
10 The most diminutive of birds, will fight,
Her young ones in her nest, against the owl.
All is the fear and nothing is the love;
As little is the wisdom, where the flight
So runs against all reason.

   Ross.   My dearest coz,
I pray you, school yourself. But, for your husband,
He is noble, wise, judicious, and best knows
The fits o'th' season. I dare not speak much further,
But cruel are the times, when we are traitors
And do not know ourselves; when we hold rumour
20 From what we fear, yet know not what we fear,
But float upon a wild and violent sea,
†Each way and none. I take my leave of you:
Shall not be long but I'll be here again:
Things at the worst will cease, or else climb upward
To what they were before. My pretty cousin,
Blessing upon you!

   L. Macduff. Fathered he is, and yet he's fatherless.

   Ross. I am so much a fool, should I stay longer
It would be my disgrace and your discomfort.
30 I take my leave at once.   *[he hurries forth*

   L. Macduff.   Sirrah, your father's dead,
And what will you do now? How will you live?

   Son. As birds do, mother.

   L. Macduff.   What, with worms and flies?

   Son. With what I get, I mean, and so do they.

   L. Macduff. Poor bird! thou'ldst never fear the net
      nor lime,
The pitfall nor the gin.

   Son. Why should I, mother? Poor birds they are not
      set for.
My father is not dead, for all your saying.

L. Macduff. Yes, he is dead: how wilt thou do for
    a father?

Son. Nay, how will you do for a husband?

L. Macduff. Why, I can buy me twenty at any market. 40

Son. Then you'll buy'em to sell again.

L. Macduff. Thou speak'st with all thy wit, and yet
    i'faith

With wit enough for thee.

Son. Was my father a traitor, mother?

L. Macduff. Ay, that he was.

Son. What is a traitor?

L. Macduff. Why, one that swears and lies.

Son. And be all traitors that do so?

L. Macduff. Every one that does so is a traitor, and
    must be hanged.   50

Son. And must they all be hanged that swear and lie?

L. Macduff. Every one.

Son. Who must hang them?

L. Macduff. Why, the honest men.

Son. Then the liars and swearers are fools; for there
are liars and swearers enow to beat the honest men
and hang up them.

L. Macduff. Now God help thee, poor monkey! But
how wilt thou do for a father?

Son. If he were dead, you'ld weep for him: if you 60
would not, it were a good sign that I should quickly
have a new father.

L. Macduff. Poor prattler, how thou talk'st!

            '*Enter a* MESSENGER'

Messenger. Bless you, fair dame! I am not to you
    known,

Though in your state of honour I am perfect.

I doubt some danger does approach you nearly.

If you will take a homely man's advice,
Be not found here; hence, with your little ones.
To fright you thus, methinks I am too savage;
70 To do worse to you were fell cruelty,
Which is too nigh your person. Heaven preserve you!
I dare abide no longer.   [*he goes*

   L. Macduff.   Whither should I fly?
I have done no harm. But I remember now
I am in this earthly world; where to do harm
Is often laudable, to do good sometime
Accounted dangerous folly: why then, alas,
Do I put up that womanly defence,
To say I have done no harm?

       '*Enter* MURDERERS'

            What are these faces?
   Murderer. Where is your husband?
80 *L. Macduff.* I hope in no place so unsanctified
Where such as thou mayst find him.
   Murderer.   He's a traitor.
   Son. Thou liest, thou †shag-haired villain.
   Murderer.   What, you egg! [*stabs him*
Young fry of treachery!
   Son.   He has killed me, mother:
Run away, I pray you.   [*dies*

     [*Lady Macduff hurries forth 'crying murder',
       pursued by the Murderers*

[4. 3.] *England. Before the palace of King Edward the
   Confessor.* MALCOLM *and* MACDUFF *come forth*

   Malcolm. Let us seek out some desolate shade, and
     there
Weep our sad bosoms empty.

Macduff.   Let us rather
Hold fast the mortal sword, and like good men
Bestride our down-fall'n birthdom: each new morn
New widows howl, new orphans cry, new sorrows
Strike heaven on the face, that it resounds
As if it felt with Scotland and yelled out
Like syllable of dolour.

  Malcolm.   What I believe, I'll wail;
What know, believe; and what I can redress,
As I shall find the time to friend, I will.   10
What you have spoke, it may be so perchance.
This tyrant, whose sole name blisters our tongues,
Was once thought honest: you have loved him well;
He hath not touched you yet. I am young, but something
      thing
You may deserve of him through me; and wisdom
To offer up a weak, poor, innocent lamb,
T'appease an angry god.

  Macduff. I am not treacherous.

  Malcolm.   But Macbeth is.
A good and virtuous nature may recoil
In an imperial charge. But I shall crave your pardon; 20
That which you are, my thoughts cannot transpose:
Angels are bright still, though the brightest fell:
Though all things foul would wear the brows of
      grace,
Yet grace must still look so.

  Macduff.   I have lost my hopes.

  Malcolm. Perchance even there where I did find my
      doubts.
Why in that rawness left you wife and child,
Those precious motives, those strong knots of love,
Without leave-taking? I pray you,
Let not my jealousies be your dishonours,

30 But mine own safeties: you may be rightly just,
Whatever I shall think.
   Macduff.   Bleed, bleed, poor country!
Great tyranny, lay thou thy basis sure,
For goodness dares not check thee: wear thou thy
      wrongs,
The title is affeered! Fare thee well, lord:
I would not be the villain that thou think'st
For the whole space that's in the tyrant's grasp,
And the rich East to boot.
   Malcolm.   Be not offended:
I speak not as in absolute fear of you:
I think our country sinks beneath the yoke,
40 It weeps, it bleeds, and each new day a gash
Is added to her wounds. I think withal
There would be hands uplifted in my right;
And here from gracious England have I offer
Of goodly thousands. But for all this,
When I shall tread upon the tyrant's head,
Or wear it on my sword, yet my poor country
Shall have more vices than it had before,
More suffer and more sundry ways than ever,
By him that shall succeed.
   Macduff.   What should he be?
50 *Malcolm*. It is myself I mean: in whom I know
All the particulars of vice so grafted
That, when they shall be opened, black Macbeth
Will seem as pure as snow, and the poor state
Esteem him as a lamb, being compared
With my confineless harms.
   Macduff.   Not in the legions
Of horrid hell can come a devil more damned
In evils to top Macbeth.
   Malcolm.   I grant him bloody,

Luxurious, avaricious, false, deceitful,
Sudden, malicious, smacking of every sin
That has a name: but there's no bottom, none,　　60
In my voluptuousness: your wives, your daughters,
Your matrons and your maids, could not fill up
The cistern of my lust, and my desire
All continent impediments would o'erbear
That did oppose my will. Better Macbeth,
Than such an one to reign.

Macduff.　　　　　　　　Boundless intemperance
In nature is a tyranny; it hath been
Th'untimely emptying of the happy throne,
And fall of many kings. But fear not yet
To take upon you what is yours: you may　　70
Convey your pleasures in a spacious plenty,
And yet seem cold, the time you may so hoodwink:
We have willing dames enough; there cannot be
That vulture in you, to devour so many
As will to greatness dedicate themselves,
Finding it so inclined.

Malcolm.　　　　　　　With this there grows
In my most ill-composed affection such
A stanchless avarice that, were I king,
I should cut off the nobles for their lands,
Desire his jewels and this other's house,　　80
And my more-having would be as a sauce
To make me hunger more, that I should forge
Quarrels unjust against the good and loyal,
Destroying them for wealth.

Macduff.　　　　　　　　This avarice
Sticks deeper; grows with more pernicious root
Than summer-seeming lust: and it hath been
The sword of our slain kings: yet do not fear;
Scotland hath foisons to fill up your will

Of your mere own. All these are portable,
90 With other graces weighed.
   Malcolm. But I have none. The king-becoming
        graces,
   As justice, verity, temp'rance, stableness,
   Bounty, perseverance, mercy, lowliness,
   Devotion, patience, courage, fortitude,
   I have no relish of them, but abound
   In the division of each several crime,
   Acting it many ways. Nay, had I power, I should
   Pour the sweet milk of concord into hell,
   Uproot the universal peace, confound
100 All unity on earth.
   Macduff.   O Scotland! Scotland!
   Malcolm. If such a one be fit to govern, speak:
   I am as I have spoken.
   Macduff.   Fit to govern!
   No, not to live. O nation miserable!
   With an untitled tyrant bloody-sceptred,
   When shalt thou see thy wholesome days again,
   Since that the truest issue of thy throne
   By his own interdiction stands accurst,
   And does blaspheme his breed? Thy royal father
   Was a most sainted king; the queen that bore thee
110 Oft'ner upon her knees than on her feet,
   Died every day she lived. Fare thee well!
   These evils thou repeat'st upon thyself
   Hath banished me from Scotland. O my breast,
   Thy hope ends here!
   Malcolm.   Macduff, this noble passion,
   Child of integrity, hath from my soul
   Wiped the black scruples, reconciled my thoughts
   To thy good truth and honour. Devilish Macbeth
   By many of these trains hath sought to win me

Into his power; and modest wisdom plucks me
From over-credulous haste: but God above   120
Deal between thee and me! for even now
I put myself to thy direction, and
Unspeak mine own detraction; here abjure
The taints and blames I laid upon myself,
For strangers to my nature. I am yet
Unknown to woman, never was forsworn,
Scarcely have coveted what was mine own,
At no time broke my faith, would not betray
The devil to his fellow, and delight
No less in truth than life: my first false speaking   130
Was this upon myself: what I am truly
Is thine and my poor country's to command:
Whither indeed, before thy here-approach,
Old Siward, with ten thousand warlike men,
Already at a point, was setting forth:
Now we'll together, and the chance of goodness
Be like our warranted quarrel! Why are you silent?

  Macduff. Such welcome and unwelcome things at
    once
'Tis hard to reconcile.

       'A Doctor' comes from the palace

  Malcolm. Well, more anon. Comes the king forth,
    I pray you?   140
  Doctor. Ay, sir: there are a crew of wretched souls
That stay his cure: their malady convinces
The great assay of art; but at his touch,
Such sanctity hath heaven given his hand,
They presently amend.
  Malcolm.   I thank you, doctor. [*the Doctor goes*
  Macduff. What's the disease he means?
  Malcolm.   'Tis called the evil:

A most miraculous work in this good king,
Which often, since my here-remain in England,
I have seen him do. How he solicits heaven,
150 Himself best knows: but strangely-visited people,
All swoln and ulcerous, pitiful to the eye,
The mere despair of surgery, he cures,
Hanging a golden stamp about their necks,
Put on with holy prayers: and 'tis spoken,
To the succeeding royalty he leaves
The healing benediction. With this strange virtue
He hath a heavenly gift of prophecy,
And sundry blessings hang about his throne
That speak him full of grace.

Ross approaches

Macduff.   See who comes here.
160 *Malcolm.* My countryman; but yet I know him not.
   Macduff. My ever gentle cousin, welcome hither.
   Malcolm. I know him now: good God, betimes
      remove
The means that makes us strangers!
   Ross.   Sir, amen.
   Macduff. Stands Scotland where it did?
   Ross.   Alas, poor country,
Almost afraid to know itself! It cannot
Be called our mother, but our grave; where nothing,
But who knows nothing, is once seen to smile;
Where sighs and groans and shrieks that rend the
      air,
Are made, not marked; where violent sorrow seems
170 A modern ecstasy: the dead man's knell
Is there scarce asked for who, and good men's lives
Expire before the flowers in their caps,
Dying or ere they sicken.

Macduff.   O, relation
Too nice, and yet too true!
    Malcolm.   What's the newest grief?
    Ross. That of an hour's age doth hiss the speaker;
Each minute teems a new one.
    Macduff.   How does my wife?
    Ross. Why, well.
    Macduff.   And all my children?
    Ross.   Well too.
    Macduff. The tyrant has not battered at their peace?
    Ross. No, they were well at peace, when I did
      leave 'em.
    Macduff. Be not a niggard of your speech: how
      goes't?   180
    Ross. When I came hither to transport the tidings
Which I have heavily borne, there ran a rumour
Of many worthy fellows that were out;
Which was to my belief witnessed the rather,
For that I saw the tyrant's power a-foot.
Now is the time of help: your eye in Scotland
Would create soldiers, make our women fight,
To doff their dire distresses.
    Malcolm.   Be't their comfort
We are coming thither: gracious England hath
Lent us good Siward and ten thousand men;   190
An older and a better soldier none
That Christendom gives out.
    Ross.   Would I could answer
This comfort with the like! But I have words,
That would be howled out in the desert air,
Where hearing should not latch them.
    Macduff.   What concern they?
The general cause? or is it a fee-grief
Due to some single breast?

Ross.   No mind that's honest
But in it shares some woe, though the main part
Pertains to you alone.
   Macduff.   If it be mine,
200 Keep it not from me, quickly let me have it.
   Ross. Let not your ears despise my tongue for ever,
Which shall possess them with the heaviest sound
That ever yet they heard.
   Macduff.   Humh! I guess at it.
   Ross. Your castle is surprised; your wife and babes
Savagely slaughtered: to relate the manner,
Were, on the quarry of these murdered deer,
To add the death of you.
   Malcolm.   Merciful heaven!
What, man! ne'er pull your hat upon your brows;
Give sorrow words: the grief that does not speak
210 Whispers the o'er-fraught heart and bids it break.
   Macduff. My children too?
   Ross.   Wife, children, servants, all
That could be found.
   Macduff.   And I must be from thence!
My wife killed too?
   Ross.   I have said.
   Malcolm.   Be comforted:
Let's make us med'cines of our great revenge,
To cure this deadly grief.
   Macduff. He has no children. All my pretty ones?
Did you say all? O, hell-kite! All?
What, all my pretty chickens and their dam
At one fell swoop?
220   *Malcolm.* Dispute it like a man.
   Macduff.   I shall do so;
But I must also feel it as a man:
I cannot but remember such things were,

That were most precious to me. Did heaven look on,
And would not take their part? Sinful Macduff,
They were all struck for thee! naught that I am,
Not for their own demerits, but for mine,
Fell slaughter on their souls: heaven rest them now!
  Malcolm. Be this the whetstone of your sword:
          let grief
Convert to anger; blunt not the heart, enrage it.
  Macduff. O, I could play the woman with mine eyes, 230
And braggart with my tongue! But, gentle heavens,
Cut short all intermission; front to front
Bring thou this fiend of Scotland and myself;
Within my sword's length set him; if he 'scape,
Heaven forgive him too!
  Malcolm.   This tune goes manly.
Come, go we to the king, our power is ready,
Our lack is nothing but our leave. Macbeth
Is ripe for shaking, and the Powers above
Put on their instruments. Receive what cheer you may;
The night is long that never finds the day.   [*they go* 240

[5. 1.] *Dunsinane. A room in the castle. 'Enter a
    Doctor of Physic, and a Waiting Gentlewoman'*

  Doctor. I have two nights watched with you, but can
perceive no truth in your report. When was it she last
walked?

  Gentlewoman. Since his majesty went into the field,
I have seen her rise from her bed, throw her night-gown
upon her, unlock her closet, take forth paper, fold it,
write upon't, read it, afterwards seal it, and again return
to bed; yet all this while in a most fast sleep.

  Doctor. A great perturbation in nature, to receive at
once the benefit of sleep and do the effects of watching! 10

In this slumbry agitation, besides her walking and other
actual performances, what, at any time, have you heard
her say?

Gentlewoman. That, sir, which I will not report after
her.

Doctor. You may to me, and 'tis most meet you should.

Gentlewoman. Neither to you nor any one, having no
witness to confirm my speech.

'Enter LADY' MACBETH, 'with a taper'

Lo you, here she comes! This is her very guise, and
20 upon my life fast asleep. Observe her, stand close.

Doctor. How came she by that light?

Gentlewoman. Why, it stood by her: she has light by
her continually, 'tis her command.

Doctor. You see, her eyes are open.

Gentlewoman. Ay, but their sense are shut.

Doctor. What is it she does now? Look, how she rubs
her hands.

Gentlewoman. It is an accustomed action with her, to
seem thus washing her hands: I have known her
30 continue in this a quarter of an hour.

Lady M. Yet here's a spot.

Doctor. Hark, she speaks! I will set down what comes
from her, to satisfy my remembrance the more strongly.

Lady M. Out, damnéd spot! out, I say! One: two:
why, then 'tis time to do't. Hell is murky! Fie, my lord,
fie! a soldier, and afeard? What need we fear who
knows it, when none can call our power to accompt?
Yet who would have thought the old man to have had
so much blood in him?

40 *Doctor.* Do you mark that?

Lady M. The Thane of Fife had a wife; where is she
now? What, will these hands ne'er be clean? No more

o'that, my lord, no more o'that: you mar all with this
starting.

Doctor. Go to, go to; you have known what you
should not.

Gentlewoman. She has spoke what she should not, I
am sure of that: heaven knows what she has known.

Lady M. Here's the smell of the blood still: all the
perfumes of Arabia will not sweeten this little hand.   50
Oh! oh! oh!

Doctor. What a sigh is there! The heart is sorely
charged.

Gentlewoman. I would not have such a heart in my
bosom, for the dignity of the whole body.

Doctor. Well, well, well,—

Gentlewoman. Pray God it be, sir.

Doctor. This disease is beyond my practice: yet I have
known those which have walked in their sleep who have
died holily in their beds.   60

Lady M. Wash your hands, put on your night-gown,
look not so pale: I tell you yet again, Banquo's buried;
he cannot come out on's grave.

Doctor. Even so?

Lady M. To bed, to bed: there's knocking at the
gate: come, come, come, come, give me your hand:
what's done, cannot be undone: to bed, to bed, to bed.

[*she goes out*

Doctor. Will she go now to bed?

Gentlewoman. Directly.

Doctor. Foul whisp'rings are abroad: unnatural deeds 70
Do breed unnatural troubles: infected minds
To their deaf pillows will discharge their secrets:
More needs she the divine than the physician:
God, God forgive us all! Look after her,
Remove from her the means of all annoyance,

And still keep eyes upon her. So, good night:
My mind she has mated and amazed my sight:
I think, but dare not speak.

 Gentlewoman.   Good night, good doctor.
                [they go

[5. 2.] *The country near Dunsinane. 'Drum and Colours. Enter MENTEITH, CAITHNESS, ANGUS, LENNOX, Soldiers'*

 Menteith. The English power is near, led on by
  Malcolm,
His uncle Siward and the good Macduff.
Revenges burn in them: for their dear causes
Would to the bleeding and the grim alarm
Excite the mortified man.

 Angus.   Near Birnam wood
Shall we well meet them, that way are they coming.

 Caithness. Who knows if Donalbain be with his
  brother?

 Lennox. For certain, sir, he is not: I have a file
Of all the gentry: there is Siward's son,
10 And many unrough youths, that even now
Protest their first of manhood.

 Menteith.   What does the tyrant?

 Caithness. Great Dunsinane he strongly fortifies:
Some say he's mad; others, that lesser hate him,
Do call it valiant fury: but, for certain,
He cannot buckle his distempered cause
Within the belt of rule.

 Angus.   Now does he feel
His secret murders sticking on his hands;
Now minutely revolts upbraid his faith-breach;
Those he commands move only in command,

Nothing in love: now does he feel his title   20
Hang loose about him, like a giant's robe
Upon a dwarfish thief.

  Menteith.   Who then shall blame
His pestered senses to recoil and start,
When all that is within him does condemn
Itself for being there?

  Caithness.   Well, march we on,
To give obedience where 'tis truly owed:
Meet we the med'cine of the sickly weal,
And with him pour we, in our country's purge,
Each drop of us.

  Lennox.   Or so much as it needs
To dew the sovereign flower and drown the weeds.   30
Make we our march towards Birnam.

                          ['*exeunt, marching*'

[5. 3.] *Dunsinane. A court in the castle.* '*Enter
      MACBETH, Doctor, and Attendants*'

  Macbeth. Bring me no more reports, let them fly all:
Till Birnam wood remove to Dunsinane
I cannot taint with fear. What's the boy Malcolm?
Was he not born of woman? The spirits that know
All mortal consequence have pronounced me thus:
'Fear not, Macbeth, no man that's born of woman
Shall e'er have power upon thee'. Then fly, false thanes,
And mingle with the English epicures:
The mind I sway by and the heart I bear
Shall never sag with doubt nor shake with fear.   10

             A '*servant*' *enters*

The devil damn thee black, thou cream-faced loon!
Where got'st thou that goose look?

Servant. There is ten thousand—

Macbeth.   Geese, villain?

Servant.   Soldiers, sir.

Macbeth. Go prick thy face and over-red thy fear,
Thou lily-livered boy. What soldiers, patch?
Death of thy soul! those linen cheeks of thine
Are counsellors to fear. What soldiers, whey-face?

Servant. The English force, so please you.

Macbeth. Take thy face hence.   [*servant goes*
         Seton!— [*brooding*] I am sick at heart,
20 When I behold—Seton, I say!—This push
Will cheer me ever, or disseat me now.
I have lived long enough: my way of life
Is fall'n into the sere, the yellow leaf,
And that which should accompany old age,
As honour, love, obedience, troops of friends,
I must not look to have; but, in their stead,
Curses, not loud but deep, mouth-honour, breath
Which the poor heart would fain deny and dare not.
Seton!

               SETON enters

30 *Seton.* What's your gracious pleasure?

Macbeth.   What news more?

Seton. All is confirmed, my lord, which was
     reported.

Macbeth. I'll fight, till from my bones my flesh be
     hacked.
Give me my armour.

Seton.   'Tis not needed yet.

Macbeth. I'll put it on.
Send out moe horses, skirr the country round,
Hang those that talk of fear. Give me mine armour....
            [*Seton goes to fetch it*
How does your patient, doctor?

Doctor.   Not so sick, my lord,
As she is troubled with thick-coming fancies,
That keep her from her rest.

Macbeth.   Cure her of that:
Canst thou not minister to a mind diseased,   40
Pluck from the memory a rooted sorrow,
Raze out the written troubles of the brain,
And with some sweet oblivious antidote
†Cleanse the stuffed bosom of that perilous stuff
Which weighs upon the heart?

Doctor.   Therein the patient
Must minister to himself.

    *Seton returns with armour and an armourer, who
        presently begins to equip Macbeth*

Macbeth. Throw physic to the dogs, I'll none of it.
Come, put mine armour on; give me my staff;
Seton, send out; doctor, the thanes fly from me;
Come, sir, dispatch.—If thou couldst, doctor, cast   50
The water of my land, find her disease,
And purge it to a sound and pristine health,
I would applaud thee to the very echo,
That should applaud again.—Pull't off, I say.—
What rhubarb, senna, or what purgative drug,
Would scour these English hence? Hear'st thou
      of them?

Doctor. Ay, my good lord; your royal preparation
Makes us hear something.

Macbeth.   Bring it after me.
I will not be afraid of death and bane
Till Birnam forest come to Dunsinane.   60

              [he goes; Seton follows with armourer

Doctor. Were I from Dunsinane away and clear,
Profit again should hardly draw me here.   *[he goes*

[5. 4.] *Country near Birnam.* '*Drum and Colours. Enter MALCOLM, SIWARD, MACDUFF, SIWARD'S Son, MENTEITH, CAITHNESS, ANGUS', LENNOX, ROSS, 'and Soldiers, marching*'

Malcolm. Cousins, I hope, the days are near at hand
That chambers will be safe.
Menteith.   We doubt it nothing.
Siward. What wood is this before us?
Menteith.   The wood of Birnam.
Malcolm. Let every soldier hew him down a bough,
And bear't before him: thereby shall we shadow
The numbers of our host, and make discovery
Err in report of us.
Soldier.   It shall be done.
Siward. We learn no other but the confident tyrant
Keeps still in Dunsinane, and will endure
10 Our setting down before't.
Malcolm.   'Tis his main hope:
For where there is advantage to be gone,
Both more and less have given him the revolt,
And none serve with him but constrainéd things
Whose hearts are absent too.
Macduff.   Let our just censures
Attend the true event, and put we on
Industrious soldiership.
Siward.   The time approaches,
That will with due decision make us know
What we shall say we have and what we owe.
Thoughts speculative their unsure hopes relate,
20 But certain issue strokes must arbitrate:
Towards which advance the war.

                          ['*exeunt, marching*'

[5. 5.] *Dunsinane. The court of the castle as before.*
'*Enter* MACBETH, SETON, *and Soldiers with Drum
and Colours*'

Macbeth. Hang out our banners on the outward walls;
The cry is still 'They come': our castle's strength
Will laugh a siege to scorn: here let them lie
Till famine and the ague eat them up:
Were they not forced with those that should be ours,
We might have met them dareful, beard to beard,
And beat them backward home.
                              ['*a cry within of women*'
                                     What is that noise?
    Seton. It is the cry of women, my good lord.   [*goes*
(*Macbeth.* I have almost forgot the taste of fears:
The time has been, my senses would have cooled   10
To hear a night-shriek, and my fell of hair
Would at a dismal treatise rouse and stir
As life were in't: I have supped full with horrors;
Direness, familiar to my slaughterous thoughts,
Cannot once start me.

                    SETON *returns*
                         Wherefore was that cry?
    Seton. The queen, my lord, is dead.
    Macbeth. She should have died hereafter;
There would have been a time for such a word.
To-morrow, and to-morrow, and to-morrow,
Creeps in this petty pace from day to day,   20
To the last syllable of recorded time;
And all our yesterdays have lighted fools
The way to dusty death. Out, out, brief candle!
Life's but a walking shadow, a poor player
That struts and frets his hour upon the stage,

And then is heard no more: it is a tale
Told by an idiot, full of sound and fury,
Signifying nothing.

'Enter a messenger'

Thou com'st to use thy tongue; thy story quickly.
30 *Messenger.* Gracious my lord,
I should report that which I say I saw,
But know not how to do't.
   Macbeth.   Well, say, sir.
   Messenger. As I did stand my watch upon the hill,
I looked toward Birnam, and anon methought
The wood began to move.
   Macbeth.   Liar and slave!
   Messenger. Let me endure your wrath, if't be not so:
Within this three mile may you see it coming.
I say, a moving grove.
   Macbeth.   If thou speak'st false,
Upon the next tree shalt thou hang alive,
40 Till famine cling thee: if thy speech be sooth,
I care not if thou dost for me as much.
†I pall in resolution, and begin
To doubt th'equivocation of the fiend
That lies like truth: 'Fear not, till Birnam wood
Do come to Dunsinane'; and now a wood
Comes toward Dunsinane. Arm, arm, and out!
If this which he avouches does appear,
There is nor flying hence nor tarrying here.
I 'gin to be aweary of the sun,
50 And wish th'estate o'th' world were now undone.
Ring the alarum bell! Blow, wind! come, wrack!
At least we'll die with harness on our back.
                           [they hurry forth

[5. 6.] *Dunsinane. Before the castle gate. 'Drum and Colours. Enter MALCOLM, SIWARD, MACDUFF, and their army, with boughs'*

Malcolm. Now near enough: your leavy screens throw
          down,
And show like those you are. You, worthy uncle,
Shall with my cousin your right noble son
Lead our first battle: worthy Macduff and we
Shall take upon's what else remains to do,
According to our order.
   Siward.   Fare you well.
Do we but find the tyrant's power to-night,
Let us be beaten, if we cannot fight.
   Macduff. Make all our trumpets speak; give them all
          breath,
Those clamorous harbingers of blood and death.   10

          They go forward, their trumpets sounding.

[5. 7.]   *MACBETH comes from the castle*

Macbeth. They have tied me to a stake; I cannot fly,
But bear-like I must fight the course. What's he
That was not born of woman? Such a one
Am I to fear, or none.

               Young SIWARD comes up

   Young Siward. What is thy name?
   Macbeth.   Thou'lt be afraid to hear it.
   Young Siward. No; though thou call'st thyself a
          hotter name
Than any is in hell.

Macbeth.   My name's Macbeth.

Young Siward. The devil himself could not pro-
        nounce a title
More hateful to mine ear.

Macbeth.   No, nor more fearful.

10 *Young Siward.* Thou liest, abhorréd tyrant, with my
        sword
I'll prove the lie thou speak'st.

        [*they 'fight, and young Siward' is 'slain'*

Macbeth.   Thou wast born of woman.
But swords I smile at, weapons laugh to scorn,
Brandished by man that's of a woman born.

*He passes on and presently a sound of more fighting
        is heard. MACDUFF comes up*

Macduff. That way the noise is. Tyrant, show thy
        face!
If thou beest slain and with no stroke of mine,
My wife and children's ghosts will haunt me still.
I cannot strike at wretched kerns, whose arms
Are hired to bear their staves; either thou, Macbeth,
Or else my sword with an unbattered edge
20 I sheathe again undeeded. There thou shouldst be;
By this great clatter, one of greatest note
Seems bruited. Let me find him, fortune!
And more I beg not. [*he follows Macbeth. 'Alarums'*

MALCOLM and old SIWARD come up

Siward. This way, my lord; the castle's gently
        rendered:
The tyrant's people on both sides do fight,
The noble thanes do bravely in the war,
The day almost itself professes yours,
And little is to do.

Malcolm.   We have met with foes
That strike beside us.
     Siward.   Enter, sir, the castle
                    [*they pass in at the gate. 'Alarum'*

[5. 8.]   *MACBETH returns*

Macbeth. Why should I play the Roman fool, and die
On mine own sword? whiles I see lives, the gashes
Do better upon them.

               MACDUFF returns, following him

Macduff.   Turn, hell-hound, turn.
Macbeth. Of all men else I have avoided thee:
But get thee back, my soul is too much charged
With blood of thine already.
     Macduff.   I have no words:
My voice is in my sword, thou bloodier villain
Than terms can give thee out! [*they 'fight'. 'Alarum'*
     Macbeth.   Thou losest labour.
As easy mayst thou the intrenchant air
With thy keen sword impress as make me bleed: 10
Let fall thy blade on vulnerable crests,
I bear a charméd life, which must not yield
To one of woman born.
     Macduff.   Despair thy charm,
And let the angel whom thou still hast served
Tell thee, Macduff was from his mother's womb
Untimely ripped.
     Macbeth. Accurséd be that tongue that tells
          me so,
For it hath cowed my better part of man!
And be these juggling fiends no more believed,
That palter with us in a double sense,   20

That keep the word of promise to our ear,
And break it to our hope. I'll not fight with thee.
  Macduff. Then yield thee, coward,
And live to be the show and gaze o'th' time.
We'll have thee, as our rarer monsters are,
Painted upon a pole, and underwrit,
'Here may you see the tyrant'.
  Macbeth.   I will not yield,
To kiss the ground before young Malcolm's feet,
And to be baited with the rabble's curse.
30 Though Birnam wood be come to Dunsinane,
And thou opposed, being of no woman born,
Yet I will try the last. Before my body
I throw my warlike shield: lay on, Macduff,
And damned be him that first cries 'Hold, enough'.
          [they fight to and fro beneath the castle wall,
             until at length 'Macbeth' is 'slain'

[5. 9.]   *Within the castle.*

'*Retreat and flourish. Enter, with Drum and Colours,*
  MALCOLM, SIWARD, ROSS, *Thanes and Soldiers*'

  Malcolm. I would the friends we miss were safe
    arrived.
  Siward. Some must go off: and yet, by these I see,
So great a day as this is cheaply bought.
  Malcolm. Macduff is missing, and your noble son.
  Ross. Your son, my lord, has paid a soldier's debt:
40 He only lived but till he was a man,
The which no sooner had his prowess confirmed
In the unshrinking station where he fought,
But like a man he died.
  Siward.   Then he is dead?

Ross. Ay, and brought off the field: your cause of
    sorrow
Must not be measured by his worth, for then
It hath no end.
    Siward.   Had he his hurts before?
Ross. Ay, on the front.
    Siward.   Why then, God's soldier be he!
Had I as many sons as I have hairs,
I would not wish them to a fairer death:
And so his knell is knolled.
    Malcolm.   He's worth more sorrow, 50
And that I'll spend for him.
    Siward.   He's worth no more.
They say he parted well and paid his score:
And so God be with him! Here comes newer comfort.

'*Enter Macduff, with Macbeth's head*'
on a pole

    Macduff. Hail, king! for so thou art. Behold, where
        stands
Th'usurper's cursèd head: the time is free:
I see thee compassed with thy kingdom's pearl,
That speak my salutation in their minds;
Whose voices I desire aloud with mine:
Hail, king of Scotland!
    All.   Hail, king of Scotland! ['*flourish*'
    Malcolm. We shall not spend a large expense of time 60
Before we reckon with your several loves,
And make us even with you. My thanes and kinsmen,
Henceforth be earls, the first that ever Scotland
In such an honour named. What's more to do,
Which would be planted newly with the time,
As calling home our exiled friends abroad
That fled the snares of watchful tyranny,

Producing forth the cruel ministers
Of this dead butcher and his fiend-like queen,
70 Who, as 'tis thought, by self and violent hands
Took off her life; this, and what needful else
That calls upon us, by the grace of Grace
We will perform in measure, time, and place:
So thanks to all at once, and to each one,
Whom we invite to see us crowned at Scone.

[*'flourish'. They march away*

GLOSSARY

Note. Where a pun or quibble is intended, the meanings are distinguished as (*a*) and (*b*).

ABSOLUTE, positive; 3. 6. 40

ACTUAL, 'exhibited in deeds' (O.E.D. 1); 5. 1. 12.

ADDITION, title; 1. 3. 106; 3. 1. 99

ADDRESS (refl.), prepare; 2. 2. 24

ADHERE, agree, suit, cohere; 1. 7. 52

ADMIRED, amazing, to be wondered at; 3. 4. 110

ADVANTAGE, favourable opportunity; 5. 4. 11

AFFECTION, disposition; 4. 3. 77

AFFEER, confirm (legally). Orig. a commercial term — fix the market price; 4. 3. 34

AGITATION, movement, activity; 'slumbry agitation' = sleep-walking; 5. 1. 11

ALARUM (vb.), call to action; 2. 1. 53

ALARUM BELL, tocsin, town or castle bell, rung in time of danger or as a call to action; (theat.) the large bell 'in the wooden tower above the tiring-house'; 2. 3. 74; 5. 5. 51

ALL-HAIL (vb.), greet with the cry 'all-hail!'; 1. 5. 6–7

ALL-THING, altogether, entirely; 3. 1. 13

AMAZE, utterly confuse (not 'astonish'); 2. 3. 108; 5. 1. 77

AMAZEDLY, 'like a man in a trance' (K.); 4. 1. 126

AMAZEMENT, stupefaction; 2. 4. 19

ANNOYANCE, harm; 5. 1. 75

ANTIC, fantastic; 4. 1. 130

ANTICIPATE, forestall; 4. 1. 144

APPLY TO, be specially directed towards; 3. 2. 30

APPROVE, prove; 1. 6. 4

ARGUMENT, subject of conversation; 2. 3. 120

AROINT, begone! (cf. *Lear*, 3. 4. 129). A word of unknown orig., only found in Sh. and his imitators; 1. 3. 6

ARTIFICIAL, produced by art (or magic); 3. 5. 27

ASSURANCE, solemn promise; 4. 1. 83

AUGER-HOLE, very small place; lit. hole made by a carpenter's auger (cf. *Cor.* 4. 6. 87); 2. 3. 122

AUGURE, divination; 3. 4. 124

AUTHORIZE, vouch for, warrant; 3. 4. 66

AVOUCH, vouch for, answer for; 3. 1. 119

BADGED, marked plainly for all to see. Retainers wore coloured 'badges' to show to whose service they belonged; 2. 3. 101

BANE, destruction; 5. 3. 59

BAREFACED, open, undisguised;
3. 1. 118

BATTLE, division of an army;
5. 6. 4

BEAR, (i) exercise, carry out,
perform; 1. 7. 17; 3. 6. 3,
17; (ii) 'bear in hand', abuse
with false pretences or ap-
pearances; 3. 1. 80

BELDAM, old woman (term of
contempt); 3. 5. 2

BELLMAN, watchman, who
called the hours and formerly
'announced deaths and called
on the faithful to pray for
the departed' (O.E.D.); 2.2.3

BENEFIT, natural advantage or
'gift' (O.E.D. 3b). Cf.
A.Y.L. 4. 1. 32; 'Disable
all the benefits of your
country'; 5. 1. 10

BENISON, blessing; 2. 4. 40

BESTOW (reflex.), lodge; 3. 1.
29; 3. 6. 24

BESTRIDE, defend a fallen friend
(cf. 1 Hen. IV, 5. 1. 122, 'if
thou see me down in the
battle and bestride me');
4. 3. 4

BILL, list; 3. 1. 99

BIRTHDOM, fatherland; 4. 3. 4

BLOOD-BOLTERED, having the
hair clotted with blood (cf.
O.E.D. balter, vb. 5. obs.
exc. in dial. 'to form tangled
knots or clots, to stick together by coagulation'); 4.
1. 123

BODEMENT, augury, presage (cf.
Troil. 5. 3. 80); 4. 1. 96

BOND, (i) life (v. note); 3.2.49;
(ii) legal agreement to fulfil
a contract; 4. 1. 84

BOTCH, 'flaw or blemish re-
sulting from unskilful work-
manship' (O.E.D.); 3. 1. 133

BREAK, impart, disclose; 1. 7. 48

BREECHED, covered (as by
breeches); 2. 3. 116

BRIEFLY, quickly; 2. 3. 133

BRINDED, early form of
'brindled'; 4. 1. 1

BROAD, free, unrestrained; 3. 4.
23; 3. 6. 21

BROIL, battle (cf. 1 Hen. IV, 1.
1. 3); 1. 2. 6

BRUIT, proclaim, announce; 5.
7. 22

BUY, acquire, win; 1. 7. 32

CARD, 'The Shipman's Card' =
the compass, lit. the circular
card with the 32 points
marked upon it; 1. 3. 17

CARELESS, uncared for, worthless, 1. 4. 11

CASE, clothe, surround; 3.4. 23

CAST, (i) (a) throw to the
ground, (b) vomit (cf. Meas.
3. 1. 92); 2. 3. 40; (ii) 'cast
the water' = diagnose by
examination of the urine;
5. 3. 50

CATCH, seize; 1. 5. 17

CAUSE, (i) business, affair; 3. 1.
33; (ii) consideration; 3. 4.
136; (iii) ground for accusa-
tion; 5. 2. 3; (iv) case, sickness; 5. 2. 15

CENSURE, judgement, opinion;
5. 4. 14

CHALLENGE, blame, accuse (cf.
Tit. And. 1. 1. 340); 3. 4. 42

CHAMBERLAIN, one who waits
on a king or lord in his bedchamber; 1. 7. 63

CHAMPION (vb.), oppose in a
'wager of battle' (cf. Ric. II,
1. 3. 5). In the sense of
'stand up, defend', the vb.
not found before 19th c.;
3. 1. 71

CHARGE (sb.), (i) office, duty, commission; 2. 2. 6; (ii) command; 4. 3. 20

CHAUDRON, entrails; 4. 1. 33

CHECK, rebuke, call to account; 4. 3. 33

CHOPPY, chapped; 1. 3. 44

CHOPS, jaws; 1. 2. 22

CHOUGH, jackdaw; 3. 4. 125

CHUCK, chick. A term of endearment (cf. *Oth.* 3. 4. 49); 3. 2. 45

CLEAR (adj. and adv.), innocent, spotless; 1. 5. 70; 1. 7. 18; 2. 1. 28

CLEARNESS, freedom from suspicion of evil; 3. 1. 132

CLEPT (p.p.), called, named; 3. 1. 93

CLING, shrivel up (cf. O.E.D. 3c); 5. 5. 40

CLOSE (vb.), (i) enclose; 3. 1. 98; (ii) heal, join; 3. 2. 14

CLOSE (adj. and adv.), secret, hidden; 3. 5. 7; 5. 1. 20

CLOUDY, angry, sullen; 3. 6. 41

COIGN, corner; 1. 6. 7

COMBINED, in collusion; 1. 3. 111

COMBUSTION, civil uproar (cf. *Hen. VIII*, 5. 4. 51); 2. 3. 58

COMMAND UPON, lay commands upon; 3. 1. 16

COMMEND, offer; 1. 7. 11

COMMISSION (in), deputed to perform a certain action; 1. 4. 2

COMPASS, surround; 5. 8. 56

COMPOSITION, agreement, peace terms; 1. 2. 61

COMPT (in), under obligation to render an account at audit-time like the steward of an estate; 1. 6. 26

CONFOUND, ruin, destroy; 2. 2. 11; 4. 1. 54; 4. 3. 99

CONFUSED, disorderly; 2. 3. 58

CONFUSION, ruin, destruction; 2. 3. 66; 3. 5. 29

CONJURE, adjure; 4. 1. 50

CONSENT, (a) collusion, complicity (cf. *A.Y.L.* 2. 2. 3), (b) counsel, advice (cf. *Wint.* 5. 3. 136); 2. 1. 25

CONSEQUENCE, future event; 1. 7. 3; 5. 3. 5

CONSTANCY, firmness of mind, courage; 2. 2. 68

CONSTRAIN, force into service, conscript; 5. 4. 13

CONSTRUCTION, interpretation; 1. 4. 12

CONTINENT, (a) containing, restraining, (b) chaste; 4. 3. 64

CONTRIVER, schemer, plotter; 3. 5. 7

CONVERT (intrans.), change; 4. 3. 229

CONVEY, contrive in secret (cf. *Lear*, 1. 2. 109—'I will convey the business as I shall find means'); 4. 3. 71

CONVINCE, overpower, defeat completely (Lat. 'convinco'); 1. 7. 64; 4. 3. 142

COPY. Either (a) copyhold, tenure (cf. 3. 2. 49) or (b) image, pattern (v. note); 3. 2. 38

CORPORAL, (i) corporeal, having a body; 1. 3. 81; (ii) bodily; 1. 7. 80

COUNTENANCE (vb.). Meaning doubtful: either (i) face, or (ii) be in keeping with, or perhaps a quibble on both; 2. 3. 80

COURSE (sb.), the onset of the dogs in bear-baiting; 5. 7. 2

Coz, 'cousin', used of any close relationship; 4. 2. 14

Crack, 'a sudden sharp and loud noise as of something breaking or bursting...formerly applied to the roar of a cannon, of a trumpet, and of thunder' (O.E.D.); 1. 2. 37; 4. 1. 117

Crave, require; 3. 1. 34

Crib, confine as in a hovel (cf. 2 Hen. IV, 3. 1. 9); 3. 4. 24

Cross, thwart; 3. 1. 80

Dainty, punctilious, particular; 2. 3. 144

Dareful (adj. or adv.), bold, defiantly; 5. 5. 6

Dear, (a) grievous, dire, (b) heart-felt, i.e. that touches closely; 5. 2. 3

Degree, rank; 3. 4. 1

Delicate, mild, pleasant; 1. 6. 10

Deliver, communicate; 1. 5. 10; 3. 3. 2

Demand, ask; 4. 1. 61

Demi-wolf, cross between wolf and dog; O.E.D. does not record elsewhere; 3.1.93

Deny, refuse; 3. 4. 128

Dignity, rank; 5. 1. 55

Direness, horror; 5. 5. 14

Discovery, reconnaissance; 5. 4. 6

Disjoint, fall to pieces; 3. 2. 16

Disorder. Either (i) agitation of mind (cf. K. John, 3. 4. 102) or (ii) commotion, confusion; 3. 4. 110

Dispatch (sb.), management (with grim pun on vb. (ii) below); 1. 5. 67

Dispatch (vb.), (i) make haste; 5. 3. 50; (ii) put to death; 3. 4. 15

Displace, banish; 3. 4. 109

Disposition, habit of mind, nature; 3. 4. 113

Dispute, resist, struggle against; 4. 3. 220

Distance, discord, variance. The orig. sense; 3. 1. 115

Distempered, diseased, distracted; 5. 2. 15

Division, variation, descant; 4. 3. 96

Doubt, fear; 4. 2. 66

Drab, strumpet; 4. 1. 31

Drenched, drowned; perhaps after 'swinish sleep' with play on 'drench' — draught or dose of medicine administered to an animal (cf. 1 Hen. IV, 2. 4. 104); 1. 7. 68

Dudgeon, haft, handle; 2. 1. 46

Dun, dark; 1. 5. 50

Duty, respect, reverence; 3. 4. 92; 4. 1. 132

Ecstasy, (i) frenzy; 3. 2. 22; (ii) excitement; 4. 3. 170

Effect, (i) fulfilment, execution; 1. 5. 46; (ii) manifestation; 5. 1. 10

Eminence, honour, distinction; 3. 2. 31

Encounter, meet, respond to; 3. 4. 9

Endure, 'suffer without opposition' (Schmidt); 5. 4. 9

Enkindle unto, 'excite...to hope for' (A. C. Bradley); 1. 3. 121

Establish (the estate), settle (the succession); 1. 4. 37

Estate, (i) government, succession to the crown; 1. 4. 37; (ii) 'th'estate of the world' — the cosmic order, the universe; 5. 5. 50

EVEN-HANDED, impartial, un-biased (cf. *Merch*. 2. 7. 25, 'weigh with even hand'); 1. 7. 10

EXPECTATION, those expected. Abstract for concrete; 3. 3. 10

EXPEDITION, haste; 2. 3. 110

FACT, evil deed, crime; 3. 6. 10

FACULTIES, powers, prero-gatives; 1. 7. 17

FANTASTICAL, imaginary; 1. 3. 53, 139

FARROW, litter of pigs; 4. 1. 65

FATAL, ominous; 2. 1. 36; 2. 2. 3; 3. 5. 21

FAVOUR, (i) indulgence; 1. 3. 149; (ii) expression; 1. 5. 71

FEE-GRIEF grief that is 'fee' or private property; 4. 3. 196

FELL (sb.), skin with hair on it, scalp; 5. 5. 11

FILE (sb.), list, catalogue; 3. 1. 94; 5. 2. 8

FILE (vb.), defile, corrupt; 3. 1. 64

FIRSTLING, first-fruit, or first-born of a flock (cf. *Deut*. xv. 19); 4. 1. 147, 148

FIT, periodical paroxysm of fever (cf. *Cor*. 3. 2. 33, 'the violent fit o'th' time'); 3. 4. 21, 55; 4. 2. 17

FITFUL, subject to fits (q.v.) or paroxysms; 3. 2. 23

FLAW, outburst, lit. gust of wind (cf. *2 Hen. IV*, 4. 4. 35); 3. 4. 63

FLIGHTY, swift, fleeting; 4. 1. 145

FLING OUT, kick out and plunge wildly; 2. 4. 16

FLOURISH, 'a fanfare of horns, trumpets, etc. to announce the approach of a person of distinction' (O.E.D.); 1. 4. 1 S.D.; 5. 8. 35 S.D.

FLOUT, insult; 1. 2. 49

FOISON, abundance; 4. 3. 88

FORCE, reinforce; 5. 5. 5

FORGE, invent, trump up; 4. 3. 82

FORK, forked tongue; 4. 1. 16

FOUNTAIN, source; 2. 3. 97

FRANCHISED, free; 2. 1. 28

FREE (vb.), banish, get rid of (cf. *Cymb*. 3. 6. 80; *Temp*. Ep. 18); 3. 6. 35

FRENCH HOSE, 'usually of mid-thigh length, shaped like pumpkins, and stuffed with hair, flocks, or bombast' (Linthicum, *Costume in Eliz. Drama*, p. 205). But the Porter seems to allude to a tighter kind; 2. 3. 13

FRET, chafe (cf. *3 Hen. VI*, 1. 4. 91); 5. 5. 25

FRUITLESS, having no issue; 3. 1. 60

FRY, spawn; 4. 2. 83

FUME, 'a noxious vapour, sup-posed formerly to rise to the brain from the stomach'; chiefly as the result of in-toxication (O.E.D.); 1. 7. 66

FUNCTION, the operation of mind or body (cf. *Oth*. 2. 3. 354); 1. 3. 140

FURY, frenzy, madness; 2. 3. 106

GALLOWGLASS, heavy-armed foot soldier from Ireland (cf. *2 Hen. VI*, 4. 9. 26); 1. 2. 13

GENIUS, guardian spirit; 3. 1. 55

GENTLE, made gentle or calm; 1. 6. 3; 3. 4. 76

GENTLY, quietly, without a struggle; 5. 7. 24

GERMEN, germ, seed (cf. *Lear*, 3. 2. 8); 4. 1. 59

GET, beget; 1. 3. 67

GIN, snare, trap; 4. 2. 35

GIVE OUT, proclaim; 4. 3. 192

GLASS, magic mirror (v. note); 4. 1. 119

Go, (i) pass, 3. 1. 91; (ii) 'go off', die (cf. *Ant.* 4. 13. 6); 5. 8. 36

GOLDEN, very favourable (cf. *A.Y.L.* 1. 1. 6, 'report speaks goldenly'); 1. 7. 33

GOOD MAN, brave man; 4. 3. 3

GOODNESS, success; 4. 3. 136

GOOSE, tailor's smoothing-iron (so called because the handle is like a goose's neck); 2. 3. 14

GOSPELLED, submissive to the gospel precepts; 3. 1. 87

GOUT, clot, thick drop; 2. 1. 46

GRACE (sb.), (i) honour, distinction; 1. 3. 55; (ii) holiness; 4. 3. 23, 24, 159

GRACE (vb.), honour; 3. 4. 41, 45

GRAFT, implant, incorporate; 4. 3. 51

GRAVE, weighty; 3. 1. 21

GRAYMALKIN, *or* Grimalkin (lit. little grey Mall or Mary), common name for a cat; 1. 1. 8

GRIPE, grasp; 3. 1. 61

GROW, (i) advance in dignity; 1. 4. 29; (ii) cling to (cf. *Hen. VIII*, 5. 5. 50, 'like a vine grow to him'); 1. 4. 32

GUISE, fashion, practice; 5. 1. 19

GULF, gullet; 4. 1. 23

HARBINGER, an officer of the royal household, who preceded the king on his journeys to procure lodgings; 1. 4. 45

HARM, evil, wickedness; 3. 5. 7; 4. 3. 55

HARNESS, armour; 5. 5. 52

HARP, guess (O.E.D. cites Cotgrave, 1611, 'to harpe at the matter'); 4. 1. 74

HARPIER, name of a demon (v. note); 4. 1. 3

HAVING (sb.), possession (cf. *Tw. Nt.* 3. 4. 343); 1. 3. 56

HEAT-OPPRESSÈD, fevered; 2. 1. 39

HEAVILY, sorrowfully; 4. 3. 182

HEAVY, drowsy (cf. *Temp.* 2. 1. 186, 191); 2. 1. 6

HECATE, goddess of the infernal region, queen of night, ghosts and magic, and guardian of witches (cf. *M.N.D.* 5. 1. 382 note); 2. 1. 52; 3. 5. 1 etc.

HERALD (vb.), usher; 1. 3. 102

HERMIT, beadsman; 1. 6. 20

HOLD, (i) keep, withhold; 3. 6. 25; (ii) entertain; 4. 2. 19

HOME (adv.), to the full; 1. 3. 120

HOMELY, humble; 4. 2. 67

HORRID, horrible; 1. 3. 135; 1. 7. 24

HOSE, breeches (v. *French hose*); 2. 3. 13

HOUSEKEEPER, watch-dog; 3. 1 96

HOWLET, owl or owlet; 4. 1. 17

HURLYBURLY, uproar, tumult; 1. 1. 3

HUSBANDRY, thrift, economy; 2. 1. 4

HYRCAN, of Hyrcania, province of Persian empire on shores of Caspian, mentioned by Pliny (*Nat. Hist.* bk. viii, c. 18) as a breeding-place for tigers; 3. 4. 101

'IELD, reward (lit. yield); 1. 6. 13

ILLNESS, evil, wickedness. The orig. sense; as 'sickness' not found before the end of 17th c.; 1. 5. 19

IMAGE, idea (cf. *M.N.D.* 5. 1. 25); 1. 3. 135

IMPRESS, conscript; 4. 1. 95

INCARNADINE, lit. make the colour of flesh, 'turn blood-red' (K.); 2. 2. 62

INDUSTRIOUS, zealous, energetic; 5. 4. 16

INFORM (v. note); 2. 1. 48

INGREDIENCE, the composition of a drug or poison, a mixture (v. note); 1. 7. 11; 4. 1. 34

INHABIT (vb.), house, harbour (v. note); 3. 4. 105

INITIATE, 'belonging to a novice or unpractised person' (O.E.D.); 3. 4. 143

INSANE, produceing insanity; 1. 3. 84

INTEMPERANCE, excess; 4. 3. 66

INTERDICTION, exclusion (v. note); 4. 3. 107

INTEREST, right or title to a share in; 1. 2. 66

INTERMISSION, delay, interval of time; 4. 3. 232

INTRENCHANT, invulnerable (cf. *trench*); 5. 8. 9

INVENTOR, contriver; 1. 7. 10

JEALOUSY, suspicion; 4. 3. 29

JUMP (vb.), risk, hazard; 1. 7. 7

JUTTY (sb.), 'projecting part of a wall or building' (O.E.D.); 1. 6. 6

KERN, light-armed foot soldier from Ireland (cf. *Ric. II*, 2. 1. 156); 1. 2. 13, 30; 5. 7. 17

LACE, 'diversify with streaks of colour' (O.E.D. 6. Cf. *Rom.* 3. 5. 8); 2. 3. 112

LAP, wrap, encase; 1. 2. 55

LARGE, unrestrained; 3. 4. 11

LATCH, catch; 4. 3. 195

LATED, belated; 3. 3. 6

LAVISH, insolent, wild (cf. *2 Hen. IV*, 4. 4. 64); 1. 2. 58

LAY ON, strike hard; 5. 8. 33

LILY-LIVERED, cowardly. The liver was the seat of courage in the old physiology; 5. 3. 15

LIMBEC, alembic, distilling vessel (full of alcoholic fumes); 1. 7. 67

LIMITED, appointed (cf. *Meas.* 4. 2. 163); 2. 3. 51

LINE, strengthen, support; 1. 3. 112

LIST, the lists; 3. 1. 70

LODGE, beat (crops) down flat; 4. 1. 55

LOON, worthless fellow; 5. 3. 11

LUXURIOUS, lascivious; 4. 3. 58

MAGGOT-PIE, magpie. Both prefixes are shortened forms of Margaret, a pet-name for the bird when caged; 3. 4. 125

MANSIONRY (collective sb.), dwellings; 1. 6. 5

MARTLET, house martin; 1. 6. 4

MATE, confound, stupefy; 5. 1. 77

MAW, stomach; 3. 4. 73; 4. 1. 23

MEASURE, proportion; 5. 8. 73

MED'CINE, doctor; 5. 2. 27

MEMORIZE, make memorable; 1. 2. 41

MERE, absolute, utter; 2. 3. 94; 4. 3. 89, 152

METAPHYSICAL, supernatural; 1. 5. 28

METTLE, life-stuff, substance, ardour, spirit; 1. 7. 73

MINION, darling, favourite, the pick of; 1. 2. 19; 2. 4. 15

MINISTER, attendant spirit (cf. *Temp.* 1. 2. 275; 3. 3. 87); 1. 5. 47

MINUTELY, every minute; 5. 2. 18

MISCHIEF, evil deed; 1. 5. 49

MISSIVE, messenger (cf. *Ant.* 2. 2. 74); 1. 5. 6

MODERN, commonplace, ordinary; 4. 3. 170

MODEST, moderate; 4. 3. 119

MORE AND LESS, high and low (cf. *2 Hen. IV*, 1. 1. 209); 5. 4. 12

MORTAL, deadly, fatal; 1. 5. 40; 3. 4. 81; 4. 3. 3

MORTALITY, human life; 2. 3. 92

MORTIFIED, dead (cf. *Caes.* 2. 1. 324; *Lear*, 2. 3. 15); 5. 2. 5

MOTIVE, incentive, person or object which prompts love, devotion, etc.; 4. 3. 27

MOULD, (a) model, pattern (tailor's), (b) bodily form (O.E.D. 10 b); 1. 3. 145

MOUSING, accustomed to prey on mice; 2. 4. 13

MOVE, disturb, agitate; 3. 4. 48

MUMMY, a common drug, orig. made from Egyptian mummies, the spices of which perhaps lent it some virtue, but often of other dead bodies. Sir Th. Browne writes: 'The common opinion of the virtues of mummy bred great consumption there-

of, and princes and great men contended for this strange panacea, wherein Jews dealt largely, manufacturing mummies from dead carcases and giving them the names of kings' (Fragment on Mummies: *Works*, ed. G. Keynes, v. 461); 4. 1. 23

MUSE, wonder; 3. 4. 85

NAPKIN, handkerchief; 2. 3. 6

NATURAL, partaking of natural or human affection; 4. 2. 9

NATURE, (i) human nature, natural habit, feeling or instinct; 1. 2. 11; 1. 3. 137; 1. 5. 49; 2. 1. 8; 2. 4. 16, 27; (ii) physical or mental constitution; (and so) vital force, life; 1. 7. 68; 2. 2. 7; 2. 3. 113; 3. 4. 28; 5. 1. 9

NAUGHT, worthless, wicked; 4. 3. 225

NAVE, navel. O.E.D. records no other instance of this meaning, though the words are etym. akin; 1. 2. 22

NEAR, nearer (cf. *Ric. II*, 5. 1. 88); 2. 3. 140

NERVE, sinew; 3. 4. 102

NICE, precise, exact; 4. 3. 174

NIGHTGOWN, dressing-gown; 2. 2. 70; 5. 1. 5

NIMBLY, briskly, breezily; 1. 6. 2

NOISE, music (cf. *Temp.* 3. 2. 133); 4. 1. 106

NONPAREIL, one who has no equal; 3. 4. 19

NOTE (sb.), (i) notoriety; 3. 2. 44; (ii) list; 3. 3. 10

NOTION, intellect, mind. The only meaning in Sh.; 3. 1. 82

OBLIVIOUS, causing oblivion; 5. 3. 43

ODDS (at), at strife; 3. 4. 127

OFFEND, irritate; 3. 4. 57

OFFERING, ceremony, ritual, prayer; 2. 1. 52

OFFICE, (i) duty, task assigned; 3. 3. 3; (ii) (plur.) servants' quarters; 2. 1. 14

OLD, plenty of, abundant (cf. *M.W.W.* 1. 4. 4); 2. 3. 2

ONCE, ever; 5. 5. 15

OUT, in the field, up in arms; 4. 3. 183

OVERCOME, come over, pass over; 3. 4. 111

OWE, own, possess; 1. 3. 76; 1. 4. 10; 3. 4. 113

PADDOCK, toad; 1. 1. 9

PAIN, trouble; 2. 3. 49

PALL, (i) shroud; 1. 5. 50; (ii) fail (cf. *Ham.* 5. 2. 9); 5. 5. 42

PALTER, shuffle, prevaricate, equivocate; 5. 8. 20

PART, depart, die; 5. 8. 52

PASS, review, go through point by point (Clar.); 3. 1. 79

PASSION, agitation, sorrowful emotion; 3. 4. 57; 4. 3. 114

PATCH, fool; 5. 3. 15

PEAK, waste away; 1. 3. 23

PENT-HOUSE, sloping roof over door or window to protect it from the weather (v. note); here, eyelid; 1. 3. 20

PERFECT, (i) reliable; 1. 5. 2; (ii) (*a*) completely satisfied (cf. *Tim.* 1. 2. 90), (*b*) whole and sound; 3. 1. 107; 3. 4. 21; (iii) fully acquainted; 4. 2. 65

PERTURBATION, disorder, anomaly; 5. 1. 9

PESTERED, harassed; 5. 2. 23

PHYSIC (vb.), 'treat with remedies, relieve, alleviate' (O.E.D.); 2. 3. 49

PITFALL, fowler's snare, 'in which a trapdoor...falls over a cavity or hollow' (O.E.D.); 4. 2. 35

PLANT, 'establish or set up (a person or thing) in some position or state' (O.E.D. 5c; cf. *L.L.L.* 1. 1. 164; *Ric. II*, 5. 1. 63; *All's Well*, 2. 3. 159); 1. 4. 28; 5. 8. 65

POINT, 'at a point', ready, fully equipped (cf. 'at point', *Lear*, 1. 4. 347; *Ham.* 1. 2. 200); 4. 3. 135

POORLY, meanly, unworthily (cf. *Ric. II*, 3. 3. 128); 2. 2. 72

PORTABLE, bearable; 4. 3. 89

POSSET, 'drink composed of hot milk curdled with ale, wine, etc. formerly used as a delicacy and as a remedy' (O.E.D.); 2. 2. 6

POST, fast-riding messenger; 1. 3. 98

POSTER, one who travels 'post', i.e. swiftly; 1. 3. 33

POWER, forces; 4. 3. 185, 236; 5. 2. 1; 5. 6. 7

PRACTICE, skill, art; 5. 1. 58

PREDOMINANCE, ascendancy. Astrol.; 2. 4. 8

PRESENT (adj.), instant; 1. 2. 66

PRETENCE, aim, intention; 2. 3. 131

PRETEND, aim at, intend; 2. 4. 24

PRIDE, highest pitch (cf. *1 Hen. IV*, 1. 1. 60); 2. 4. 12

PROBATION, proof (cf. *Meas.* 5. 1. 156); 3. 1. 79

Produce forth, bring to light; 5. 8. 68

Profess, claim knowledge or skill in; 4. 1. 50

Profound, deep-hanging, 'and therefore ready to fall' (Clar.); 3. 5. 24

Proof, impenetrable armour; 1. 2. 55

Proper, fine (contemptuous); 3. 4. 60

Proportion, adjustment, proportioning (O.E.D. 6); 1. 4. 19

Prospect, the range of vision; 1. 3. 74

Prosperous, profitable; 3. 1. 21

Protest, proclaim; 3. 4. 105; 5. 2. 11

Provoke, stimulate; 2. 3. 26

Purge (sb.), cleansing, purification (by blood-letting). Not in O.E.D., but v. *2 Hen. IV*, 4. 1. 65, 'Purge the obstructions which begin to stop Our very veins of life', and *Ric. II*, 1. 1. 153; 5. 2. 28

Purge (vb.), purify by purgative; 5. 3. 52

Purveyor, officer sent on in advance to provide food for the king and his retinue; 1. 6. 22

Push, attempt, crisis (cf. *Ham.* 5. 1. 289, 'put the matter to the present push'); 5. 3. 20

Pyramid, spire; 4. 1. 57

Quarrel, cause; 1. 2. 14

Quarry, heap of slaughtered deer at the end of a chase (cf. *Ham.* 5. 2. 362); 4. 3. 206

Question, discuss; 2. 3. 128

Rancour, malicious enmity; 3. 1. 66

Rapt, lost in reverie; 1. 3. 57, 142; 1. 5. 5

Ravelled, tangled. knotted; 2. 2. 37

Ravin up, swallow up greedily (cf. 'ravin down', *Meas.* 1. 2. 125); 2. 4. 28

Ravined, glutted, (or) ravenous (v. note); 4. 1. 24

Rawness, unprotected condition (cf. O.E.D. 'raw' 6, excoriated, and *Hen. V*, 4. 1. 139–40, 'children rawly left'); 4. 3. 26

Raze out, erase, blot out; 5. 3. 42

Rebuke, repress (cf. *K. John* 2. 1. 9); 3. 1. 55

Receipt, receptacle, container; 1. 7. 66

Receive, believe, accept as true; 1. 7. 74, 77

Recoil, give way suddenly (like a spring or a gun); 4. 3. 19; 5. 2. 23

Recommend (refl.), make itself agreeable; 1. 6. 2

Reflection, shining; 1. 2. 25

Relation, recital; 4. 3. 173

Relish, trace, hint; 4. 3. 95

Remembrancer, one engaged or appointed to remind another; 3. 4. 37

Remorse, pity (cf. *Temp.* 5. 1. 76), relenting (cf. *Merch.* 4. 1. 20); 1. 5. 43

Render, surrender; 5. 7. 24

Repeat, recite; 4. 3. 112

Repetition, report, account; 2. 3. 84

Resolve (refl.), make up one's mind; 3. 1. 138

Rest, remain; 1. 6. 20

RETREAT, a signal on the trumpet to recall a pursuing force (cf. *2 Hen. IV*, 4. 3. 70); 5. 8. 34 S.D.

RONYON. A term of abuse, lit. scabby, mangy (cf *M.W.W.* 4. 2. 180); 1. 3. 6

ROUND, (i) crown; 1. 5. 29; 4. 1. 88; (ii) round dance; 4. 1. 130

ROUSE, bestir oneself, rise up; 3. 2. 53; 5. 5. 12

RUB, roughness, unevenness. A term of bowls (cf. *Ham.* 3. 1. 65); 3. 1. 133

RUGGED, (i) 'wrinkled with care or displeasure; frowning' (O.E.D. 3b); 3. 2. 27; (ii) rough, shaggy; 3. 4. 100

RUIN, destruction, death; 2. 3. 114

RUMP-FED. Either, fed on rump, the best beef, or, fat-rumped (for 'fed' = fattened, v. O.E.D.); 1. 3. 6

SAG, sink 'through lack of strength or effort' (O.E.D. 2); 5. 3. 10

SAUCY, (i) importunate, pushing; 3. 4. 25; (ii) impertinent; 3. 5. 3

SCAN, examine, consider; 3. 4. 140

SCARF UP, blindfold; 3. 2. 47

SCHOOL (vb.), control, discipline; 4. 2. 15

SCORCH, slash, cut; 3. 2. 13

SCORE, reckoning, debt; 5. 8. 52

SCOUR, wash away purge; 5. 3. 56

SCRUPLE, doubt; 2. 3. 129

SEASON, that which keeps things fresh, preservative; 3. 4. 141

SEAT, situation; 1. 6. 1

SEATED, firmly fixed (cf. 'the seated hills', *Par. Lost*, vi, 644); 1. 3. 136

SECURITY, over-confidence; 3. 5. 32

SEEL, blind. Lit. sew (a falcon's) eyelids together; 3. 2. 46

SELF-ABUSE, hallucination (cf. *Ham.* 4. 7. 49); 3. 4. 142

SELF-COMPARISONS, qualities equal to his own (cf. *Ant.* 3. 13. 26); 1. 2. 56

SENNET, flourish on a trumpet; 3. 1. 10 S.D.

SENSE, apprehension; 5. 1. 25

SENSIBLE TO, perceptible by; 2. 1. 36

SERE (sb.), withered state; 5. 3. 23

SET, (i) stake; 3. 1. 112; (ii) 'set forth', display; 1. 4. 6; (iii) 'set down before', besiege (cf. *Cor.* 1. 2. 28); 5. 4. 10

SETTLED, determined, resolute; 1. 7. 79

SEV'NIGHT, week; 1. 3. 22

SEWER, 'attendant at a meal who superintended the arrangement of the table, the seating of the guests, and the tasting and serving of the dishes' (O.E.D.); 1. 7 S.D.

SHARD-BORNE, supported on 'shards' = scaly wing-cases (cf. note); 3. 2. 42

SHIFT (vb.) 'shift away', slip away unobserved; 2. 3. 145.

SHIFT (sb.) 'make a shift' = manage somehow or other; 2. 3. 40

SHOUGH, shag-haired kind of dog; 3. 1. 93

SIGHTLESS, invisible; 1. 5. 48; 1. 7. 23

Single, feeble; 1. 3. 140 (with quibble on 'single' = individual); 1. 6. 16

Skipping, light-footed; 1. 2. 30

Skirr, scour; 5. 3. 35

Slab (adj.), viscous, glutinous; 4. 1. 32

Sleave, filaments of silk (v. note); 2. 2. 37

Sleek (vb.), smoothe. Gen. applied to the hair; 3. 2. 27

Sliver, tear off a twig (cf. *Lear*, 4. 2. 34); 4. 1. 28

Slope, bend (v. note); 4. 1. 57

Sole, mere; 4. 3. 12

Solely, absolutely, entirely; 1. 5. 69

Solemn, official, ceremonial; 3. 1. 14

Sooth, true; 5. 5. 40

Sore, dreadful; 2. 4. 3

Sorry, woeful, wretched; 2. 2. 20, 21; 3. 2. 9

Speculation, power of sight, 'intelligent or comprehending vision' (O.E.D.; cf. *Troil.* 3. 3. 109); 3. 4. 95

Spongy, soaked to capacity (with drink); 1. 7. 71

Sprite, spirit; 2. 3. 79; 4. 1. 127

Spy. Meaning doubtful (v. note); 3. 1. 129

Staff, lance (lit. shaft); 5. 7. 18

Stamp, coin (cf. *M.W.W.* 3. 4. 16); 4. 3. 153

Stanchless, insatiable (cf. *Tit. And.* 3. 1. 14); 4. 3. 78

Stand, (i) 'stand upon', be particular about, insist upon; 3. 4. 119; (ii) 'stand to 't', (*a*) be resolute, (*b*) fall to work (cf. *Temp.* 3. 3. 49); 3. 3. 15

Start (sb.), impulse. As we now say 'fits and starts' (cf.

Lear, 1. 1. 304, 'such unconstant starts'); 3. 4. 63

Start (vb.), (i) jump from its place; 4. 1. 116; 5. 2. 23; (ii) startle, cause to start; 5. 5. 15

State, (i) 'state of man' = (*a*) all the mental and physical attributes of manhood, (*b*) the 'little kingdom' (*Caes.* 2. 1. 67–8; cf. *K. John*, 4. 2. 245–6); 1. 3. 140; (ii) chair of state (cf. *1 Hen. IV*, 2. 4. 372, 'this chair shall be my state'); 3. 4. 5

Station, place, position; 3. 1. 101; 5. 8. 42

Stay, await; 4. 3. 142

Stick deep, go deep; 3. 1. 49; 4. 3. 85

Still, always; 3. 1. 21

Straight, immediately; 3. 1. 139

Strange, (i) unaccustomed, unfamiliar; 1. 3. 145; (ii) astonished as at something new or strange; 3. 4. 112

Study, 'to be studied in' = to have got up a part perfectly; 1. 4. 9

Suborn, procure one to do an evil action; 2. 4. 24

Sudden, impetuous, violent (cf. *A.Y.L.* 2. 7. 151); 4. 3. 59

Suggestion, prompting, temptation; 1. 3. 134

Summons, call to surrender (to sleep); 2. 1. 6

Surcease, discontinuance, death; 1. 7. 4

Surmise, speculation; 1. 3. 141

Survey, perceive, notice; 1. 2. 31

Sway, direct my actions, control myself; 5. 3. 9

SWELL, overflow, burst forth
(cf. 'swelling', full to bursting, *1 Hen. IV*, 3. 1. 199;
Tit. And. 5. 3. 13); 1. 2. 28

SWELLING, increasing (in gran-
deur or greatness); 1. 3. 128

SWELTERED, 'exuded like sweat
as if by heat' (O.E.D.); 4. 1. 8.

SWOOP, (a) pounce, (b) sweep of
the stakes; 4. 3. 219

TAINT, be infected with; 5. 3. 3

TAKE OFF, kill, destroy; 3. 1.
104; 5. 8. 71

TAKING-OFF, murder; 1. 7. 20

TEEM, bring forth (cf. *Hen. V*,
5. 2. 51); 4. 3. 176

TEMPERANCE, moderation, self-
control; 4. 3 92

TEMPERATE, self-controlled; 2.
3. 108

THICK-COMING, coming rapidly
(one after the other; cf. 1. 3.
97); 5. 3. 38

THOUGHT, 'upon a thought'
= as quick as thought, in an
instant; 3. 4. 55

TIME, world, society; 1. 5. 62,
63; 1. 7. 81; 4. 3. 72

TITLE, possession; 4. 2. 7

TOUCH, feeling (cf. *Temp.* 5. 1.
21); 4. 2. 9

TOWER, 'mount up, as a hawk,
so as to be able to swoop
down on the quarry'
(O.E.D.); 2. 4. 12

TOY, trifle; 2. 3. 93

TRACE, follow; 4. 1. 153

TRADE, have dealings with; 3.
5. 4

TRAIN, false lure, lit. carrion
dragged or distributed in a
line to lure wild beasts into
a trap; 4. 3. 118

TRAMMEL UP, enmesh. A trammel = a very effective net

(for fish or fowl) in mesh of
two sizes, by means of which
the prey securely noosed
itself in a bag; 1. 7. 3

TRANSPORT, carry away by
violent emotion; 1. 5. 55

TRANSPOSE, change; 4. 3. 21

TREATISE, discourse, story; 5.
5. 12

TRENCH, cut; 3. 4. 27

TRIFLE, make trivial by com-
parison; 2. 4. 4

TUG, pull about roughly, maul;
3. 1. 111

UNBEND, slacken, relax (cf.
'bend up', 1. 7. 79); 2. 2.
45

UNDEEDED, without having
achieved any deed; 5. 7. 20

UNFIX, loosen (cf. *2 Hen. IV*,
4. 1. 208); 1. 3. 135

UNMAKE, undo, ruin (O.E.D.
3); 1. 7. 54

UNMANNERLY, immodestly; 2.
3. 116

UNROUGH, unbearded, smooth-
faced; 5. 2. 10

UNSEAM, rip up; 1. 2. 22

UNTITLED, having no claim (to
the throne); 4. 3. 104

UPROAR (vb.), throw into confusion. Not found else-
where; 4. 3. 99

USE (sb.), normal operation;
1. 3. 137

USE (vb.), keep company with;
3. 2. 10

UTTERANCE. 'A challenge or a
combat "à l'outrance", to
extremity, was a fixed term
of the law of arms, when the
combatants engaged "with
an odium internecinum", an
intention to destroy each
other' (J.); 3. 1. 71

VALUED FILE, catalogue raisonné (Clar.), priced catalogue (Steevens); 3. 1. 94

VANTAGE, favourable opportunity or position; 1. 2. 31; 1. 3. 113; 1. 6. 7

VAULT, (a) cavern, cellar, (b) the earth (with sky as roof); 2. 3. 95

VIRTUE, healing power; 4. 3. 156

VISIT, afflict with disease; 4. 3. 150

VISITING (sb.), access of feeling; 1. 5. 44

VIZARD, mask; 3. 2. 34

VOLUME, space; 2. 4. 2

VOUCH, lit. warrant (a legal term); hence, back or recommend by words of welcome; 3. 4. 34

WAKE, arouse; 3. 6. 31

WANTON, capricious, unrestrained; 1. 4. 34

WARRANT (sb.), justification; 2. 3. 145

WARRANT (vb.), justify; 4. 3. 137

WASSAIL, carousal; 1. 7. 64

WASTEFUL, laying waste, devastating; 2. 3. 114

WATCH (vb.), sit up at night; 5. 1. 1

WATCHER (v. watch); 2. 2. 71

WATCHING (sb.), being awake; 5. 1. 10

WATER-RUG, rough-haired water dog; 3. 1. 93

WEAL, society, commonwealth; 3. 4. 76; 5. 2. 27

WEIRD, having to do with fate or destiny; 1. 3. 32 (v. note); 1. 5. 8; 2. 1. 20; 3. 1. 2; 3. 4. 133; 4. 1. 136

WELL, probably, very likely (cf. mod. 'it may well be that...'); 5. 2. 6

WHILE, till; 3. 1. 43

WIN, win over, gain one's confidence; 1. 3. 123, 125

WINK AT, shut one's eyes to; 1. 4. 52

WITHERED, 'gaunt, spectre-like' (Schmidt); 1. 3. 40; 2. 1. 52

WORM, serpent, snake; 3. 4. 29

WROUGHT, exercised, agitated; 1. 3. 149

YESTY, frothy, foaming; 4. 1. 53

WORDSWORTH CLASSICS

General Editors: Marcus Clapham & Clive Reynard

JANE AUSTEN
Emma
Mansfield Park
Northanger Abbey
Persuasion
Pride and Prejudice
Sense and Sensibility

ARNOLD BENNETT
Anna of the Five Towns

R. D. BLACKMORE
Lorna Doone

ANNE BRONTË
Agnes Grey
*The Tenant of
Wildfell Hall*

CHARLOTTE BRONTË
Jane Eyre
The Professor
Shirley
Villette

EMILY BRONTË
Wuthering Heights

JOHN BUCHAN
Greenmantle
Mr Standfast
The Thirty-Nine Steps

SAMUEL BUTLER
The Way of All Flesh

LEWIS CARROLL
Alice in Wonderland

CERVANTES
Don Quixote

G. K. CHESTERTON
*Father Brown:
Selected Stories*
*The Man who was
Thursday*

ERSKINE CHILDERS
The Riddle of the Sands

JOHN CLELAND
*Memoirs of a Woman of
Pleasure: Fanny Hill*

WILKIE COLLINS
The Moonstone
The Woman in White

JOSEPH CONRAD
Heart of Darkness
Lord Jim
The Secret Agent

J. FENIMORE COOPER
*The Last of the
Mohicans*

STEPHEN CRANE
*The Red Badge of
Courage*

THOMAS DE QUINCEY
*Confessions of an English
Opium Eater*

DANIEL DEFOE
Moll Flanders
Robinson Crusoe

CHARLES DICKENS
Bleak House
David Copperfield
Great Expectations
Hard Times
Little Dorrit
Martin Chuzzlewit
Oliver Twist
Pickwick Papers
A Tale of Two Cities

BENJAMIN DISRAELI
Sybil

THEODOR DOSTOEVSKY
Crime and Punishment

**SIR ARTHUR CONAN
DOYLE**
*The Adventures of
Sherlock Holmes*
*The Case-Book of
Sherlock Holmes*
*The Lost World &
Other Stories*
*The Return of
Sherlock Holmes*
Sir Nigel

GEORGE DU MAURIER
Trilby

ALEXANDRE DUMAS
The Three Musketeers

MARIA EDGEWORTH
Castle Rackrent

GEORGE ELIOT
The Mill on the Floss
Middlemarch
Silas Marner

HENRY FIELDING
Tom Jones

F. SCOTT FITZGERALD
*A Diamond as Big as the
Ritz & Other Stories*
The Great Gatsby
Tender is the Night

GUSTAVE FLAUBERT
Madame Bovary

JOHN GALSWORTHY
In Chancery
The Man of Property
To Let

ELIZABETH GASKELL
Cranford
North and South

KENNETH GRAHAME
*The Wind in the
Willows*

**GEORGE & WEEDON
GROSSMITH**
Diary of a Nobody

RIDER HAGGARD
She

THOMAS HARDY
*Far from the
Madding Crowd*
The Mayor of Casterbridge
*The Return of the
Native*
Tess of the d'Urbervilles
The Trumpet Major
*Under the Greenwood
Tree*

This edition published 1992
by Wordsworth Editions Limited
Cumberland House, Crib Street, Ware,
Hertfordshire SG12 9ET

ISBN 1-57335-378-8

*Printed and bound in Great Britain
by Mackays of Chatham plc, Chatham, Kent*